W9-ATG-778

Toddler Storytimes II

Diane Briggs

Illustrations by Thomas Briggs

THE SCARECROW PRESS, INC.
Lanham, Maryland • Toronto • Plymouth, UK
2008

SCARECROW PRESS, INC.

Published in the United States of America
by Scarecrow Press, Inc.
A wholly owned subsidiary of The Rowman & Littlefield Publishing Group, Inc.
4501 Forbes Boulevard, Suite 200, Lanham, Maryland 20706
www.scarecrowpress.com

Estover Road
Plymouth PL6 7PY
United Kingdom

British Library Cataloguing in Publication Information Available

Library of Congress Cataloging-in-Publication Data

Briggs, Diane.
    Toddler storytimes II / Diane Briggs ; illustrations by Thomas Briggs.
        p. cm.
    Includes bibliographical references and index.
    ISBN-13: 978-0-8108-6057-5 (pbk. : alk. paper)
    ISBN-10: 0-8108-6057-0 (pbk. : alk. paper)
    eISBN-13: 978-0-8108-6228-9
    eISBN-10: 0-8108-6228-X
    1. Storytelling. 2. Children's stories. 3. Flannel boards. 4. Early childhood education—
Activity programs. I. Briggs, Thomas, ill. II. Title.
    LB1140.35.S76B753 2008
    372.67'7—dc22   2008006243

6691

∞™ The paper used in this publication meets the minimum requirements of American National
Standard for Information Sciences—Permanence of Paper for Printed Library Materials,
ANSI/NISO Z39.48-1992.
Manufactured in the United States of America.

To my lovely little niece, Andrea

Contents

Acknowledgments....................................vii

Introduction...ix

1 Bunnies, Eggs, and Chicks 1

2 Farmyard Fun 7

3 Feathered Friends................................13

4 Fish Stories...17

5 Funny Ducks 23

6 Going to the Zoo..................................27

7 Hugs and Kisses..................................35

8 I'm a Little Pumpkin............................41

9 Let's Count..49

10 Little, Adorable Me 55

11 Monkeyshines 59

12 My Daddy and I 65

13 My Mommy and I 71

14 Noisy Stories 75

15 Nursery Rhyme Time 83

16 Out Came the Sun...............................91

17 A Rainbow of Colors 95

18 Ruff! Ruff!...101

19 Silly Stuff...109

20 Squeak and Meow.............................111

21 Teddy Bear Dance.............................117

22 Turtles and Frogs...............................123

23 Vroom! Zoom! Things That Go..............129

24 What'll We Do with the Baby-O?............133

25 Yummers 143

Song Discography 147

Bibliography 151

Index 157

About the Author and Illustrator 165

Acknowledgments

Many thanks to all the librarians and storytellers I've known over the years from whom I've learned so much. I'd also like to acknowledge the youth services departments of the Bethlehem Public Library in Delmar, New York, and the Guilderland Public Library in Guilderland, New York. Perusing their children's picture-book collections helped me to choose some of the great books for the twenty-five themed programs featured in this book. Kind thanks also go to Debbie Sternklar, for sharing with me her wonderful techniques for creating attractive flannel-board figures through the use of fusible web and other interesting materials. Because so much of this book is devoted to flannel-board storytelling, her ideas are an excellent addition. The fingerplays, poems, stories, and songs in this book were either collected from folklore by unknown authors or written by myself unless otherwise indicated. Every effort has been made to identify unknown authors, and any copyright omission or credit not given is unintentional. Gracious thanks go to my editor, Kim Tabor, for being patient while I changed my mind several times about what type of book I wanted to write. Another big thank-you goes to my husband, Scott, for supporting me while I worked on this project. Finally, extreme thanks go to my son, Tom, for creating the wonderful illustrations. You are fantastic!

Introduction

The wonderful world of toddler storytime is filled with stories, songs, puppets, fingerplays, and all things charming and magical. Beyond that, the benefits to the child are enormous. Research on early childhood brain development clearly shows the supreme importance of this type of programming. Toddler programs set the stage for the development of increased attention spans, superior language development, and a love of literature and libraries. Parents and other caregivers benefit also as they gather ideas for more learning activities at home. The repetition of fingerplays, songs, and stories further enhances a child's cognitive development. Parents will also enjoy the opportunity to meet other parents of toddlers to compare notes, lend support, and develop friendships. To give an example of how beneficial library programming can be, a friend of mine told me of how her daughter, as a little child, couldn't get enough of library storytimes. She begged her mother to take her to as many storytimes as possible, and now, lo and behold, she is a graduate of Harvard and a doctor.

Drawing from my experience in toddler programming, I have put together twenty-five themes that are part of a toddler's world. It is my hope that these programs will help you to create successful storytimes that are a joy and a delight to all.

Planning Tips

- Be prepared. Make sure you have familiarized yourself with the books, fingerplays, songs, flannel-board stories, and so on that you will use in the storytime. Take a little time to practice things out loud.
- Use a planning sheet to write down the elements of your storytime in a sequential form.
- Parents or other caregivers must be present during toddler storytime.
- Keep the storytime group size to about fifteen.
- Read with expression and take your time. Be sure to give the children enough time to take in the illustrations.
- Keep each activity short. Your storytime should contain about ten components.
- Use opening and closing songs to ease transitions.
- Your program should last about twenty minutes or, with a craft activity, about forty minutes.
- Repeat rhymes and fingerplays.
- Use attention grabbers such as songs, puppets, pop-up books, and fingerplays throughout your storytime.

Suggested Books

For each of the twenty-five themes in this book, I have listed an abundance of high-quality titles that will work well with toddlers. The usual number of books shared in toddler storytime is two or three, but to allow for personal preference and availability, I have purposely provided more titles than you can use in one session. Pop-up and lift-a-flap books are superb attention getters, and I have included many of these in the lists. Big books are also especially effective. Use these whenever you can. As we all know, toddlers love to touch things, so consider purchasing several copies of high-quality touch and feel books. An example of this genre is *That's Not My Teddy*, which is one of the many titles by Fiona Watt. Let the toddlers and caregivers follow along with their own copies as you read aloud. What could be more satisfying for toddlers than to experience the joy of hearing a story while also touching and feeling it? In the end, choose the books that you love best and this will come across to the children. The results will be joyful, successful storytimes.

Fingerplays

Fingerplays are indispensable in toddler storytimes. Toddlers love them and delight in doing them over and over again. Choose favorites that work well for you, and repeat them in every program. Fingerplays focus attention at the beginning of a storytime and hold things together throughout. They work quite well as transitions between stories and help to release pent-up energy. As an added benefit, when you perform fingerplays, you are perpetuating a treasured folk tradition. Included with each theme are several coordinating fingerplays and rhymes for you to choose from.

Flannel-Board Activities

Presenting stories on a flannel board is a wonderful storytelling tradition that children and adults love. Storytellers throughout time have used figures and cut-outs to tell stories, and this medium holds the attention of toddlers quite effectively. Every theme in this book includes a flannel-board story or poem, and the patterns for these can be found at the end of each section.

Creating Flannel-Board Figures

There are many ways to create attractive flannel-board figures. I would like to suggest a few easy methods that are fun and that produce very appealing results. Many storytellers use felt, non-fusible interfacing, or Pellon to make story figures. These are all found in fabric stores. Nonfusible interfacing and Pellon are easy to use because these fabrics are semitransparent and as easy to cut as paper. Trace the story-figure patterns onto the fabric using a Sharpie or similar marker. Before cutting the figures out, color them with high-quality colored pencils or fabric paint. To complete the figures, glue on eyes, craft hair, sequins, or whatever else strikes your fancy. If the figures need to stick to each other or overlap during the storytelling, use felt instead of Pellon. Felt should also be used for larger pieces such as trees or houses to ensure they will stick to the board.

Another easy way to create story figures is by using fusible web, which is available in fabric and craft stores. Normally used in quilting or appliqué work, fusible web is a paper-backed adhesive that is semitransparent. Use it to add clothing pieces or other accents to story figures without worrying about the messiness or drying time of glue. Place the fusible web over a story-figure pattern (rough side down) and trace it. Cut a circle around the tracing. Next, iron the fusible web (rough side down) to the wrong side of a piece of fabric. For example, if you are making a zebra, use a fabric that has zebra stripes. Or, if you're making a pair of pants for a story figure, use corduroy or some other fabric. Now, cut the figure out. Next, peel off the paper backing and iron the figure (sticky side down) to a piece of felt or, in the case of clothing, iron it onto a figure that has been traced on felt but not cut out. It is best to cut out figures after ironing to prevent the heated glue from getting on your ironing board or iron. Carefully cut the excess felt from the edges of the figure. Paint or glue on other embellishments as needed. Give this easy method a try, and have fun!

Additional Tips

- Use sharp scissors.
- Use flexible fabric glue, such as Aleene's Tacky Glue.
- Use sticky-back felt (found in fabric and craft stores) to create interior lines in story figures, such as a chicken wing outline, a smile, eyebrows, or a cat's whiskers.
- Look for interesting fabrics that feature pictures of such things as teddy bears, dinosaurs, sea creatures, jungle animals, or whatever goes with the story ideas you have in mind. Use fusible web to back the fabric pictures with felt.
- Be as creative as you like, and add materials such as craft hair, wiggle eyes, sequins, or feathers to your story figures.
- Be sure to enlarge the patterns in this book as needed to coordinate with the size of your flannel board and to make them easily visible from a distance.

Puppets

Nearly every theme in this book contains suggestions for incorporating puppets. Puppets make marvelous little hosts and can be used to introduce a storytime, sing songs, or act out a simple story or rhyme. They put toddlers at ease, focus their attention, and create a warm, nonthreatening link between child and storyteller. A soft cuddly puppet is a wonderful help with transitions. When storytime is over, a puppet can sing a good-bye song and leave everyone with good feelings by giving out hugs at the end of the program.

Music

Toddlers love music, and it is essential to incorporate it into your storytime. If your group seems restless, a song is the perfect way to draw them in. Use a cute puppet to sing a silly song. Play an instrument such as a guitar or autoharp, or sing along to a CD. Give toddlers egg shakers to shake along to songs such as "Shake My Sillies Out" on Raffi's *More Singable Songs* CD, or "Shake It Up" on Katherine Dines's *Hunk-Ta-Bunk-Ta Funsies 2.* (Most upbeat songs will work with shakers.) Every theme in this book includes suggestions for several songs. For your convenience, all songs are also listed in a discography at the end of the book.

Finally, be sure to use opening and closing songs. This routine will help toddlers feel secure and make transitions easier. The following are suggestions for opening songs (see the discography near the end of the book for more choices):

- "The More We Get Together"
- "So Happy You're Here"
- "Good Morning, Merry Sunshine"

And here are some suggestions for closing songs (again, see the discography for other options):

- "Storytime Is over Now"
- "Skinnamarink"
- "Goodbye Song"

Crafts

It's not necessary to provide a craft activity to have successful storytimes. However, the toddlers and caregivers will love the opportunity to create a craft together whenever you can offer one. The craft activities in this book have been designed with simplicity and safety in mind. Small craft items that can be swallowed have been avoided, and the use of washable glue sticks and washable markers is recommended. A simple craft makes a nice ending to a program. Toddlers will delight in showing off their projects and will be happy to have something to take home.

CHAPTER 1

Bunnies, Eggs, and Chicks

Decorate your story area with stuffed toy bunnies, chicks, and colored eggs in baskets. Introduce the storytime with a bunny puppet and have him or her act out the rhyme "Here Is a Bunny." Present the story *The Singing Chick* on the flannel board and, for more fun, show the toddlers and caregivers how to make a cute egg bunny.

Suggested Books

Brown, Margaret Wise. *The Golden Egg Book*. New York: Golden, 1947.

Denchfield, Nick. *Charlie Chick: A Pop-Up Book*. New York: Red Wagon, 2007.

Gag, Wanda. *ABC Bunny*. New York: Coward, McCann and Geoghegan, 1933.

Ginsburg, Mirra. *Good Morning, Chick*. New York: Greenwillow, 1980.

Lawrence, John. *This Little Chick*. Cambridge, Mass.: Candlewick, 2002.

O'Keefe, Susan Heyboer. *Love Me, Love You*. Honesdale, Pa.: Boyds Mills, 2001.

Roddie, Shen. *Hatch, Egg, Hatch!* Boston: Little, Brown, 1990.

Van Laan, Nancy. *Scrubba Dub*. New York: Atheneum, 2003.

Watt, Fiona. *That's Not My Bunny*. Tulsa, Okla.: Usborne, 2005.

Wells, Rosemary. *Read to Your Bunny*. New York: Scholastic, 1997.

Willems, Mo. *Knuffle Bunny: A Cautionary Tale*. New York: Hyperion, 2004.

Fingerplays and Rhymes

Hop, Little Bunny
(folk rhyme; suit actions to words)

Hop, little bunny, hop, hop, hop.
Hop, little bunny, don't you stop.
Hop, little bunny, one, two, three.
Hop, little bunny, hop to me.

Here Is a Bunny
(folk rhyme)

Here is a bunny with ears so funny,
(hold up two bent fingers)
And here is his home in the ground.
(make a circle with thumb and index finger of
   other hand)
When a noise he hears, he pricks up his ears,
(straighten fingers)
And he jumps to his home in the ground.
(two fingers dive into circle of other hand)

(Idea: Use a bunny puppet to act out the rhyme.)

A Perfect White Egg
(folk rhyme)

A perfect white egg sat on by Mother Hen
To keep it warm and then,
Crack, crack, crack,
Peep, peep, peep,
A baby chick softly cheeps.

(Puppet idea: Place a pom-pom chick, or one made of felt, inside a plastic egg. Use a chicken puppet to play the part of Mother Hen. Open the egg on cue as you say the rhyme. This is a good way to introduce any of the books about chicks listed in this section.)

Let Me Hear You

Let me hear you peep like a chick.
Let me see you hop like a bunny.
Let me hear you cock-a-doodle doo.
Now be as quiet as an egg, thank you.

Songs

The song "Baby Chickie" can be found on the CD *So Big: Activity Songs for Little Ones* by Hap Palmer. Act out a hatching chick when you play or sing this song. In addition, the *Happy Easter Songs* CD from Sony Music has many songs about eggs and bunnies, including "The Funny Little Bunny."

Flannel-Board Story: *The Singing Chick*

The Singing Chick by Victoria Stenmark is the story of a just-hatched, happy little chick who loves to sing. Unfortunately, she gets swallowed by a fox, who then gets swallowed by a wolf, who then gets swallowed by a bear. However, all ends well.

Directions

Obtain a copy of the book and learn the story. Cut a hill shape from a large piece of felt. Before beginning the story, set up the scene. Place the hill in the middle of the board, with the tree next to it. Place the chick on the flannel board and cover the chick with the egg shell. Describe the cracking of the egg and remove the egg shell. When an animal is swallowed, quickly grab it off the board, hiding it from view. At the end of the story, move the bear to the top of the hill to illustrate his skipping, and then position him to show how he fell and crashed against the tree. Return the swallowed animals to the board as they pop out of the bear's stomach.

Craft: Egg Bunny

Let parents and other caregivers help the toddlers glue bunny features onto plastic eggs. Provide them with precut construction-paper ears, whiskers, noses, eyes, and paws. Provide pom-poms for tails. A strip of heavy paper with the ends taped together will form a ring that can be used as a base for the bunny egg.

Supplies

Plastic eggs
Construction paper
Washable glue sticks
Pom-poms
Washable markers

CHAPTER 2

Farmyard Fun

Dress up in a straw hat, red handkerchief, and overalls and enjoy stories, songs, and activities full of farmyard fun and frolic. Use a farm-animal puppet host, such as a pig, a cow, or a lamb, to introduce stories and activities and sing farm songs. Sing "Had a Little Rooster" while placing cute farm animals on the flannel board, and then show parents and toddlers how to make a funny rooster craft.

Suggested Books

Carroll, Kathleen Sullivan. *One Red Rooster.* Boston: Houghton Mifflin, 1992.

Cimarusti, Marie Torres. *Peek-a-Moo!* New York: Dutton Children's Books, 1998.

Denchfield, Nick. *Charlie Chick: A Pop-Up Book.* New York: Red Wagon, 2007.

Faulkner, Keith. *The Long-Nosed Pig.* New York: Dial Books for Young Readers, 1998.

Fleming, Denise. *Barnyard Banter.* New York: Holt, 1994.

Kutner, Merrily. *Down on the Farm.* New York: Holiday House, 2004.

Most, Bernard. *Cock-a-Doodle-Moo!* San Diego, Calif.: Harcourt Brace, 1996.

Smee, Nicola. *Clip-Clop.* New York: Boxer, 2006.

Steer, Dugald. *Snappy Little Farmyard: Spend a Day Down on Noisy Farm.* Brookfield, Conn.: Millbrook, 1999.

Tafuri, Nancy. *Early Morning in the Barn.* New York: Greenwillow, 1983.

Tafuri, Nancy. *Spots, Feathers, and Curly Tails.* New York: Greenwillow, 1988.

Wojtowycz, David. *Can You Moo?* New York: Scholastic, 2003.

Fingerplays and Rhymes

On the Farm
(folk rhyme)

Here is the piggy snout;
(hold up thumb)
He'd better stop eating, or his tail will pop out!
Here is busy Mother Hen;
(hold up pointer finger)
She likes to scratch for her chickens ten.
Here is patient, friendly cow;
(hold up middle finger)
She's eating hay from a big haymow.
Here is Baa-Baa, a wooly sheep;
(hold up ring finger)
Her wool keeps me warm while I am asleep.
Here is funny, fuzzy cat;
(hold up little finger)
She likes to chase a mouse or rat.

(Idea: This rhyme may also be used with finger puppets or the flannel board.)

The Boy in the Barn
(folk rhyme)

A little boy went into a barn,
(hold up index finger)
And lay down on some hay.
(lay finger down on other hand)
An owl came out, and flew about,
(cross wrists and thumbs and flap fingers)
And the little boy ran away.
(hide index finger behind back)

Songs

Hey, Diddle, Diddle
(nursery song)

Hey diddle, diddle,
The cat and the fiddle,
The cow jumped over the moon;
The little dog laughed
To see such a sport,
And the dish ran away with the spoon.

Baa, Baa, Black Sheep
(nursery song)

Baa, baa, black sheep,
Have you any wool?
Yes! Sir. Yes! Sir.
Three bags full;
One for my master,
One for my dame,
And one for the little boy
Who lives down the lane.

(Additional songs: You'll find "Down on Grandpa's
Farm" on the CD *One Light, One Sun* by Raffi.
"Old MacDonald Had a Farm" is on the CD *101
Toddler Favorites* from Music for Little People.)

Flannel-Board Song

Had a Little Rooster
(traditional; see song discography for tune)

Had a little rooster by the barnyard gate.
That little rooster was my playmate.

That little rooster went cock-a-doodle-doo,
Dee-doodle-dee, doodle-dee, doodle-dee-doo.

Had a little cat by the barnyard gate.
That little cat was my playmate.
That little cat went meow, meow, meow.
That little rooster went cock-a-doodle-doo,
Dee-doodle-dee, doodle-dee, doodle-dee-doo.

Had a little dog by the barnyard gate.
That little dog was my playmate.
That little dog went arf, arf, arf.
That little cat went meow, meow, meow.
That little rooster went cock-a-doodle-doo,
Dee-doodle-dee, doodle-dee, doodle-dee-doo.

Had a little duck by the barnyard gate.
That little duck was my playmate.
That little duck went quack, quack, quack.
That little dog went arf, arf, arf.
That little cat went meow, meow, meow.
That little rooster went cock-a-doodle-doo,
Dee-doodle-dee, doodle-dee, doodle-dee-doo.

Had a little pig by the barnyard gate.
That little pig was my playmate.
That little pig went oink, oink, oink.
That little duck went quack, quack, quack.
That little dog went arf, arf, arf.
That little cat went meow, meow, meow.
That little rooster went cock-a-doodle-doo,
Dee-doodle-dee, doodle-dee, doodle-dee-doo.

Had a little sheep by the barnyard gate.
That little sheep was my playmate.
That little sheep went baa, baa, baa.
That little pig went oink, oink, oink.
That little duck went quack, quack, quack.
That little dog went arf, arf, arf.
That little cat went meow, meow, meow.
That little rooster went cock-a-doodle-doo,
Dee-doodle-dee, doodle-dee, doodle-dee-doo.

Had a little cow by the barnyard gate.
That little cow was my playmate.
That little cow went moo, moo, moo.
That little sheep went baa, baa, baa.
That little pig went oink, oink, oink.
That little duck went quack, quack, quack.

That little dog went arf, arf, arf.
That little cat went meow, meow, meow.
That little rooster went cock-a-doodle-doo,
Dee-doodle-dee, doodle-dee, doodle-dee-doo.

Had a little horse by the barnyard gate.
That little horse was my playmate.
That little horse went neigh, neigh, neigh.
That little cow went moo, moo, moo.
That little sheep went baa, baa, baa.
That little pig went oink, oink, oink.
That little duck went quack, quack, quack.
That little dog went arf, arf, arf.
That little cat went meow, meow, meow.
That little rooster went cock-a-doodle-doo,
Dee-doodle-dee, doodle-dee, doodle-dee-doo.

Directions

Add each animal to the flannel board in succession as you sing the song. Use the cat and dog patterns from the "Feathered Friends" storytime (chapter 3) and use the sheep and cow patterns from the "Hugs and Kisses" storytime (chapter 7).

Craft: Paper-Cup Rooster

In this activity, parents and other caregivers help toddlers glue precut construction-paper pieces onto cups to make funny roosters. To make each rooster, turn a paper cup over and glue on yellow paper beaks, red paper combs, feather wings and tails, and paper eyes. Poke two holes near the rim of the cup and push in two feet made of pipe cleaners. Take a small length of pipe cleaner and twist it around a longer length to make three toes.

Supplies

Paper cups (white, brown, or yellow)
Construction paper
Feathers
Washable glue sticks
Pipe cleaners (yellow)

CHAPTER 3

Feathered Friends

njoy these fantastic stories and fun finger-plays about our feathered friends. Act out "Two Little Redbirds" with finger puppets and then repeat it as a fingerplay. Sing bird songs and present the story "The Big Fat Worm" on the flannel board. Next, show how to make a beautiful feathered-friend craft.

Suggested Books

Baker, Keith. *Big Fat Hen*. San Diego, Calif.: Harcourt Brace, 1994.

Barry, Frances. *Duckie's Rainbow*. Cambridge, Mass.: Candlewick, 2004.

Demarest, Chris. *Honk!* Honesdale, Pa.: Boyds Mills, 1998.

Ehlert, Lois. *Feathers for Lunch*. San Diego, Calif.: Harcourt Brace Jovanovich, 1990.

Fox, Mem. *Boo to a Goose*. New York: Dial, 1998.

Halpern, Shari. *Little Robin Redbreast*. New York: North-South, 1994.

Hutchins, Pat. *Rosie's Walk*. New York: Macmillan, 1968.

Tafuri, Nancy. *Silly Little Goose!* New York: Scholastic, 2001.

Tafuri, Nancy. *Whose Chick Are You?* New York: Greenwillow, 2007.

Waddell, Martin. *Owl Babies*. Cambridge, Mass.: Candlewick, 1992.

Fingerplays and Rhymes

Two Little Redbirds
(folk rhyme)

Two little redbirds
Sitting on a hill,
One named Jack,
(hold up right index finger)
One named Jill.
(hold up left index finger)
Fly away Jack,
(hide right hand behind back)
Fly away Jill.
(hide left hand behind back)
Come back Jack,
(bring right finger back)
Come back Jill.
(bring left finger back)

(Puppet idea: Use finger puppets to perform this rhyme.)

Here Is a Nest for a Robin
(folk rhyme)

Here is a nest for a robin
(cup hands)
And here is a hive for a bee
(close fist)

And here is a hole for a bunny
(make a circle with both hands)
And here is a house for me.
(make roof with both hands/arms over head)

Little Birds Fly
(folk rhyme)

Up, up in the sky, the little birds fly.
(fingers flying like birds)
Down, down in the nest, the little birds rest.
(hands form nest)
With a wing on the left, and a wing on the right,
(tuck thumbs under armpits)
Let the little birds rest all night.
(head to one side and close eyes as if sleeping)
The bright sun comes up, the dew falls away,
(touch fingers over head and flutter fingers
    down)
Good morning, good morning, the little birds say.
(form hands like beaks and open and shut them)

Songs

Sing a Song of Sixpence
(traditional; see song discography for tune)

Sing a song of sixpence,
A pocket full of rye;
Four and twenty blackbirds
All baked in a pie.

When the pie was opened,
The birds began to sing;
Wasn't that a dainty dish
To set before the King?

The King was in his counting-house,
Counting out his money;
The Queen was in the parlor,
Eating bread and honey.

The maid was in the garden,
Hanging out the clothes,
When down came a blackbird
And snipped off her nose!

Bluebird
(traditional; see song discography for tune)

Bluebird, bluebird, through my window.
Bluebird, bluebird, through my window.
Bluebird, bluebird, through my window.
Hey, diddle-dum a day day.

(Additional songs: On the CD *You Are My Little Bird* by Elizabeth Mitchell you'll find plenty of bird songs, such as "Little Bird, Little Bird," "Three Little Birds," and "Little Wing.")

Flannel-Board Story

The Big Fat Worm by Nancy Van Laan is a story about what happens when a big fat bird tries to eat a big fat worm.

Directions

Use the tree pattern from the "Bunnies, Eggs, and Chicks" storytime. Place each story figure on the flannel board on cue according to the story. When the worm goes underground, remove it from the board. When the bird flies away, remove it from the board. Place the cat in the tree when the dog chases it.

Craft: Feathered Friend

To prepare for the craft, cut bird shapes from heavy paper. Let parents and other caregivers help the toddlers decorate the bird with markers and glue on feathers. As a final touch, ask the caregivers to tape a craft stick to the bottom of the bird so each toddler can hold a bird up high and show it off.

Supplies

Heavy paper
Washable glue sticks
Feathers
Craft sticks
Washable markers

CHAPTER 4

Fish Stories

Enjoy stories of whoppers and underwater adventures. Introduce the storytime with a fish or sea-creature puppet. Have the puppet sing along to a recording of "Three Little Fishies," and give the toddlers egg shakers to shake to the music. Next, show the kids how to go fishing in a wading pool and catch some magnetic fish. If you still have time for more fun, do the "fish with shiny scales" craft.

Suggested Books

Barner, Bob. *Fish Wish*. New York: Holiday House, 2000.

Carle, Eric. *Mr. Seahorse*. New York: Philomel, 2004.

Cousins, Lucy. *Hooray for Fish!* Cambridge, Mass.: Candlewick, 2005.

Kalan, Robert. *Blue Sea*. New York: Scholastic, 1979.

MacDonald, Suse. *Sea Shapes*. San Diego, Calif.: Harcourt Brace, 1994.

Van Laan, Nancy. *Little Fish Lost*. New York: Atheneum, 1998.

Wood, Audrey. *Ten Little Fish*. New York: Blue Sky, 2004.

Wu, Norbert. *Fish Faces*. New York: Holt, 1993.

Fingerplays and Rhymes

Five Little Fishes
(adapted folk rhyme)

Five little fishes
(hold up five fingers and count down as fish
    disappear)
Swimming in the sea,
Teasing Mr. Crocodile,
You can't catch me.
(wag one finger)
Along comes Crocodile
(form crocodile jaws with two hands)
As quiet as can be . . .
SNAP!
(clap hands shut)

Four little fishes
(hold up four fingers)
Swimming in the sea,
(finish the verse as above)

(Continue until there are no fish left . . . "No little fishes swimming in the sea." Change the crocodile to a shark or octopus if desired.)

Catching a Fish
(Mother Goose)

One, Two, Three, Four, Five,
(count fingers on left hand)
I caught a little fish alive.
(catch fingers on right hand with left hand)
Why did you let it go?
(release fingers quickly)
Because it bit my fingers so.
(shake right hand)
Which finger did it bite?
The little finger on the right.
(point to little finger on right hand)

Slippery Fish
(folk rhyme)

Slippery fish, slippery fish,
(place palms together and make wavy swimming
    motions)
Sliding through the water.
Slippery fish, slippery fish,
(wavy motions)
Glub, glub, glub.
(open and close palms; repeat)

Songs

Three Little Fishies
(by Josephine Judson Carringer;
see song discography for tune)

Down in the meadow in a little bitty pool
Swam three little fishies and a mama fishie too.
"Swim," said the mama fishie, "Swim if you can,"
And they swam and they swam all over the dam.
Boop boop dit-tem dat-tem what-tem Chu!
Boop boop dit-tem dat-tem what-tem Chu!
Boop boop dit-tem dat-tem what-tem Chu!
And they swam and they swam all over the dam.

"Stop," said the mama fishie, "or you will get
    lost."
The three little fishies didn't wanna be bossed.
The three little fishies went off on a spree,
And they swam and they swam right out to
    the sea.
Boop boop dit-tem dat-tem what-tem Chu!

Boop boop dit-tem dat-tem what-tem Chu!
Boop boop dit-tem dat-tem what-tem Chu!
And they swam and they swam right out to
    the sea.

"Whee!" yelled the little fishies, "Here's a lot
    of fun.
We'll swim in the sea till the day is done."
They swam and they swam, and it was a lark
Till all of a sudden they saw a shark!
Boop boop dit-tem dat-tem what-tem Chu!
Boop boop dit-tem dat-tem what-tem Chu!
Boop boop dit-tem dat-tem what-tem Chu!
Till all of a sudden they saw a shark!

"Help!" cried the little fishies, "Gee! look at all
    the whales!"
And quick as they could, they turned on their
    tails
And back to the pool in the meadow they swam,
And they swam and they swam back over
    the dam.
Boop boop dit-tem dat-tem what-tem Chu!
Boop boop dit-tem dat-tem what-tem Chu!
Boop boop dit-tem dat-tem what-tem Chu!
And they swam and they swam back over
    the dam.

(Idea: Give the toddlers egg shakers to shake
along to the song as you sing or play a recording
of the music.)

(Additional songs: You'll find "Baby Beluga" on
Raffi's CD *Raffi on Broadway*. Other selections are
the Beatles' "Octopus's Garden" and Disney's
"Under the Sea" from the *Little Mermaid* CD.)

Activity: Go Fish

Make twenty or more fish out of heavy paper of
different colors, and decorate attractively. There
should be one fish for each child. Stick inexpen-
sive magnets on the fish. Place them in a child's
wading pool (without water). Make fishing poles
using cardboard tubes and yarn. Tie large paper
clips to the end of the yarn. Let the toddlers take
turns fishing, and allow each child to take a pole
and one fish home.

Treats

To end the fishing activity, offer a snack of goldfish crackers and juice. Small cups of blue Jell-O in clear cups with gummy fish set in the gelatin are also a fun treat option.

Flannel-Board Poem

Red Fish, Red Fish

Red Fish, Red Fish, what do you see,
Way down deep in the deep, blue sea?
I see a yellow starfish looking at me.
Yellow Starfish, Yellow Starfish, what do you see,
Way down deep in the deep, blue sea?
I see a pink seahorse looking at me.

Pink Seahorse, Pink Seahorse, what do you see,
Way down deep in the deep, blue sea?
I see a green turtle looking at me.

Green Turtle, Green Turtle, what do you see,
Way down deep in the deep blue sea?
I see a purple octopus looking at me.

Purple Octopus, Purple Octopus, what do
    you see,
Way down deep in the deep, blue sea?
I see a blue shark looking at me! Swim away!
    Swim away!

Blue Shark, Blue Shark, what do you see,
Way down deep in the deep, blue sea?
I see I'm ALL ALONE (sigh) in the deep,
    blue sea.

Directions

Place the sea creatures on the flannel board on cue according to the poem. After the shark appears, remove all creatures except the shark.

Craft: Fish with Shiny Scales

To prepare for the craft, cut fish shapes (enough for all participants) from heavy paper. Cut scales from several different colors of shiny wrapping paper. Let the toddlers glue the shiny scales onto the fish shapes. Caregivers can use markers to add eyes and a mouth.

Supplies

Heavy paper
Shiny wrapping paper
Washable glue sticks
Washable markers

CHAPTER 5

Funny Ducks

"He led the others with a quack, quack, quack!" These stories and activities are just ducky. Introduce the storytime with a duck puppet and have it act out the rhyme "Funny Ducky." You could also have it sing any or all of the duck songs featured. "The Little White Duck" flannel-board song is a charming old favorite that caregivers and toddlers will love. As for the craft, what could be cuter than a mother duck and ducklings?

Suggested Books

Barry, Frances. *Duckie's Rainbow*. Cambridge, Mass.: Candlewick, 2004.

Barry, Frances. *Duckie's Splash*. Cambridge, Mass.: Candlewick, 2006.

Ford, Bernette G. *No More Diapers for Ducky*. London: Boxer, 2006.

Hindley, Judy. *Do Like Duck Does*. Cambridge, Mass.: Candlewick, 2002.

Simmons, Jane. *Daisy's Hide-and-Seek: A Lift-the-Flap Book*. Boston: Little, Brown, 2001.

Tafuri, Nancy. *Goodnight, My Duckling*. New York: Scholastic, 2005.

Thompson, Kim Mitzo. *Six Little Ducks (Sing-a-Story)*. Columbus, Ohio: School Specialty, 2006.

Thompson, Lauren. *Little Quack*. New York: Little Simon, 2005.

Wellington, Monica. *All My Little Ducklings*. New York: Dutton, 1995.

Yolen, Jane. *Dimity Duck*. New York: Philomel, 2006.

Fingerplays and Rhymes

Funny Ducky
(folk rhyme)

Waddle, waddle, waddle ducky,
Waddle to the pond.
(place thumbs in armpits and act like a duck)
Paddle, paddle, paddle ducky,
Paddle round and round.
(paddle with hands)
Tail up, head down, funny little duck,
Tail up, head down, funny little duck.
(move head downward and place hands behind back to represent tail)

(Puppet idea: Act out this rhyme with a duck puppet.)

Five Little Ducks Went in for a Swim
(folk rhyme)

Five little ducks went in for a swim;
(hold up five fingers)
The first little duck put his head in.
(put head down)

The second little duck put his head back;
(bring head back)
The third little duck said, Quack, quack, quack.
(do quacking motion with hand)
The fourth little duck, with his tiny brother,
Went for a walk with his father and mother.
(walk fingers up arm)

Songs

Five Little Ducks
(traditional; see song discography for tune)

Five little ducks
Went out one day,
Over the hills and far away.
Mother duck said,
"Quack, quack, quack, quack."
But only four little ducks came back.
(repeat with three, two, and one)
Sad mother duck
Went out one day,
Over the hills and far away.
The sad mother duck said,
"Quack, quack, quack, quack."
And all of the five little ducks came back!

Six Little Ducks
(traditional; see song discography for tune)

Six little ducks
That I once knew,
Fat ones, skinny ones,
Fair ones too.

But the one little duck
With the feather on his back,
He led the others with a quack, quack, quack!
Quack, quack, quack! Quack, quack, quack!
He led the others with a quack, quack, quack!

Down to the river
They would go,
Wibble-wobble, wibble-wooble,
To and fro.

But the one little duck
With the feather on his back,
He led the others with a quack, quack, quack!
Quack, quack, quack! Quack, quack, quack!
He led the others with a quack, quack, quack!

(Additional song: Raffi sings "Ducks Like Rain" on his CD *Rise and Shine* from Rounder Records.)

Flannel-Board Song

The song "The Little White Duck" can be found on the CD *Everything Grows* by Raffi.

Directions

Place a green felt lily pad on the flannel board before beginning the song. Sing "The Little White Duck" as you place the story figures on the board in succession as they appear in the song. By the end of the song, all the creatures are removed from the board except the lily pad. The toddlers and adults will love this old favorite.

Craft: Mother Duck and Ducklings

Let the toddlers glue precut duck shapes to a construction-paper background. Glue yellow feathers to the ducks, and add details with crayons.

Supplies

Precut mother duck and several ducklings for
    each child
Construction paper
Feathers
Washable glue sticks
Crayons

CHAPTER 6

Going to the Zoo

Enjoy these wonderful stories about animals of all kinds. When you read *From Head to Toe* by Eric Carle, encourage the toddlers to perform the same actions as the animals in the book. It's a great way for them to learn about the different parts of the body. Have fun presenting the wonderful story *Sam Who Never Forgets* on the flannel board. To end the program, make lion masks.

Suggested Books

Cabrera, Jane. *Rory and the Lion*. New York: DK Publishing, 1999.

Campbell, Rod. *Dear Zoo*. New York: Four Winds, 1983.

Carle, Eric. *From Head to Toe*. New York: HarperCollins, 1997.

Cimarusti, Marie Torres. *Peek-a-Zoo!* New York: Dutton, 2003.

Ehlert, Lois. *Color Zoo*. New York: Lippincott, 1989.

Hort, Lenny. *We're Going on a Safari*. New York: Harry N. Abrams, 2002.

Leslie, Amanda. *Flappy, Waggy, Wiggly*. New York: Dutton, 1999.

Martin, Bill. *Polar Bear, Polar Bear, What Do You Hear?* New York: Holt, 1991.

Rathmann, Peggy. *Good Night, Gorilla*. New York: Putnam, 1994.

Rice, Eve. *Sam Who Never Forgets*. New York: Morrow, 1977.

Tafuri, Nancy. *Spots, Feathers, and Curly Tails*. New York: Greenwillow, 1988.

Walsh, Melanie. *Do Monkeys Tweet?* Boston: Houghton Mifflin, 1997.

Fingerplays and Rhymes

Spotted Giraffe
(folk rhyme)

The spotted giraffe is tall as can be,
(raise one arm high)
His lunch is a bunch of leaves off a tree,
(nibble with fingers of hand of raised arm)
He has a very long neck and his legs are
    long too,
(point to raised arm and legs)
And he can run faster than his friends at the zoo!
(run in place)

Elephant Walks
(folk rhyme)

The elephant walks
Like this and like that.
(sway back and forth with your hands clasped
    together to represent trunk)
He's terribly big,
(stretch arms up)

And he's terribly fat.
(stretch arms out)
He has no fingers,
(wiggle your fingers)
But he does have toes,
(point to your toes)
And, goodness gracious,
What a nose!
(extend one arm out in front of nose and wave
    it around)

Five Little Monkeys
(folk rhyme)

Five little monkeys,
(hold up hand to show five fingers)
Swinging in a tree,
Teasing Mr. Crocodile,
Can't catch me, can't catch me.
(shake one finger)
Along comes Crocodile,
(form crocodile jaws with hands)
Quiet as can be,
And SNAPS that monkey
(snap hands shut)
Right out of that tree!
(repeat for four little monkeys, then three, two,
    and one)
Oh, oh. No more monkeys swinging in a tree.

(Puppet idea: Use monkey finger puppets and a
crocodile hand puppet to perform this rhyme.)

Songs

You'll find the song "Going to the Zoo" on the
Peter, Paul, and Mommy CD by Peter, Paul, and
Mary. "At the Zoo" is on the CD *Wee Sing Animals, Animals, Animals*.

Flannel-Board Story

Sam Who Never Forgets by Eve Rice is the story of
a zookeeper who never forgets to feed his animals. One day the elephant thinks Sam forgot
him, but all ends well.

Directions

Obtain a copy of the book and learn the story. To
begin the story, place Sam on the flannel board
with his wagon full of animal food. Place each
animal in front of Sam on cue, and put the food
on each animal's mouth. Remove Sam and his
wagon from the board when he exits to get the
elephant's hay. Place the elephant on the board,
and tell the part in the story where the elephant
is worried that Sam forgot him. To end the story,
bring Sam back with a wagonload of hay.

Craft: Lion Mask

To prepare for the craft, cut eye holes in yellow
paper plates. Let caregivers and toddlers glue on
yarn or shredded paper for a mane, along with
construction-paper ears and pipe-cleaner whiskers.
Other details can be added with washable markers.

Supplies

Yellow paper plates
Washable glue sticks
Yarn or shredded paper
Construction paper
Pipe cleaners
Washable markers

CHAPTER 7

Hugs and Kisses
A Valentine's Day Storytime

Enjoy stories about hugs and kisses that will touch your heart. Use little heart-shape finger puppets to do the rhyme "Valentine Hearts." Present the classic story *Ask Mr. Bear* on the flannel board, and help the caregivers and toddlers create a funny heart puppet to take home.

Suggested Books

Alborough, Jez. *Hug*. Cambridge, Mass.: Candlewick, 2000.

Genechten, Guido van. *Because I Love You So Much*. Wilton, Conn.: Tiger Tales, 2004.

Karas, Brian G. *Skidamarink: A Silly Love Song to Sing Together*. New York: HarperFestival, 2002.

Katz, Karen. *Counting Kisses*. New York: McElderry, 2001.

Katz, Karen. *Daddy Hugs*. New York: Little Simon, 2007.

Katz, Karen. *Mommy Hugs*. New York: McElderry, 2006.

Katz, Karen. *Where Is Baby's Valentine?* New York: Little Simon, 2006.

Lawrence, Michael. *Baby Loves*. New York: DK Publishing, 1999.

Miller, Virginia. *I Love You Just the Way You Are*. Cambridge, Mass.: Candlewick, 1998.

O'Keefe, Susan Heyboer. *Love Me, Love You*. Honesdale, Pa.: Boyds Mills, 2001.

Thompson, Lauren. *Mouse's First Valentine*. New York: Simon and Schuster, 2002.

Fingerplays and Rhymes

Little Heart
(folk rhyme)

I have a little heart
(place hand over heart)
That goes thump, thump, thump.
(pat chest three times)
It keeps right on beating
When I jump, jump, jump.
(jump three times)
I get a special feeling
When I look at you.
(point to child)
It makes me want to give you
A kiss or two.
(blow kisses)

Valentine in a Box
(folk rhyme)

Valentine in a Box sits so still.
(crouch down)
Won't you come out? Yes, I will!
(jump up)

Valentine Hearts

Beautiful, red valentines, how many do you see?
Valentines, valentines, can you count them all
    with me?
One for Daddy, one for Mommy,
(hold one finger up at a time)
One for little Sue,
One for Bonnie, one for Tommy,
And here is one for you!
(form a heart with thumbs and index fingers)

(Idea: Place heart shapes on the flannel board or use little heart-shape felt finger puppets to present this rhyme.)

Songs

Skinnamarink
(traditional; see song discography for tune)

Skinnamarink e-dink e-dink
Skinnamarink e-doo
I love you.
Skinnamarink e-dink e-dink
Skinnamarink e-doo
I love you.
I love you in the morning
And in the afternoon.
I love you in the evening
Underneath the moon.
Oh, Skinnamarink e-dink e-dink
Skinnamarink e-doo
I love you.
I do.

(Additional music: "All You Need Is Love" can be found on the CD *All You Need Is Love* from Music for Little People. "Magic Penny," also called "Love Is Something If You Give It Away," can be found on the CD *A Cathy and Marcy Collection for Kids* by Cathy Fink.)

Flannel-Board Story

Ask Mr. Bear by Marjorie Flack is the story of a little boy who is searching for a present for his mother. He asks several different animals for advice and finally gets a great suggestion from a bear. To adapt the book for a Valentine's Day theme, say that the boy is hunting for a Valentine's Day present for his mother instead of a birthday present.

Directions

Obtain a copy of the book and learn the story. When making the boy story figure, add details to both sides of the figure so the boy can face either direction. He will be facing the animals when talking to them, and in some scenes the animals will be following behind him. When the boy goes to find the bear, remove all the other animals from the board. Have the boy hug the mother at the end of the story.

    Note: Another wonderful story to use with the flannel board that also works well with the "Hugs and Kisses" theme is *A Kiss for Little Bear*. The directions and patterns are in chapter 21.

Craft: Funny Heart Puppet

Let parents and other caregivers help toddlers draw faces on big red hearts. Use white yarn pieces to create arms and legs. Glue the arms to the sides of the heart and the legs to the bottom. Glue small hearts to the ends of the yarn pieces to create feet and hands. Finally, glue on a craft stick so the puppet can be held up and jiggled, causing the arms and legs to dance around.

Supplies

Red heavy paper
Washable markers or crayons
White yarn
Craft sticks
Washable glue sticks

CHAPTER 8

I'm a Little Pumpkin

This storytime is full of playful pumpkins. Decorate the room with jack-o-lanterns and painted pumpkins. Perform the rhyme "Bumpity Pumpkin" with a pumpkin stick puppet. Sing pumpkin songs and present the rhyme "Five Little Pumpkins in a Pumpkin Patch" on the flannel board. To end the storytime, show how to make a peek-a-boo pumpkin puppet.

Suggested Books

Hall, Zoë. *It's Pumpkin Time*. New York: Scholastic, 1994.

Hill, Eric. *Spot's Halloween*. New York: Putnam, 2003.

Holub, Joan. *Eek-A-Boo! A Spooky Lift-a-Flap Book*. New York: Scholastic, 2000.

Katz, Karen. *Where Is Baby's Pumpkin? A Lift-the-Flap Book*. New York: Little Simon, 2006.

Scott, Michael. *Five Little Pumpkins*. New York: Hyperion, 2003.

Titherington, Jean. *Pumpkin, Pumpkin*. New York: Greenwillow, 1986.

Van Rynbach, Iris. *Five Little Pumpkins*. Honesdale, Pa.: Boyds Mills, 1995.

Fingerplays and Rhymes

I'm a Little Pumpkin
(folk rhyme; tune: "I'm a Little Teapot")

I'm a little pumpkin,
Fat and round,
(hold arms out to indicate roundness)
Sitting in a pumpkin patch,
(squat down)
On the ground.
I can be a jack-o-lantern
With two big eyes
(circle eyes with fingers)
Or made into a big fat pie.
(make pie shape with arms)

Bumpity Pumpkin

Bumpity Pumpkin
Sat on a wall,
(place a fist or pumpkin puppet on top of
    one arm)
Bumpity Pumpkin
Took a great fall.
(fist or puppet "falls" off arm)
There he goes
Bumping down the street,
(bump fist or puppet along arm)

Bumpity Pumpkin
Trick or Treat!

(Puppet idea: Perform this rhyme with a pumpkin stick puppet.)

Five Little Pumpkins
(folk rhyme)

Five little pumpkins sitting on a gate,
The first one said, "Oh, my it's getting late!"
The second one said, "There are witches in
   the air."
The third one said, "But we don't care."
The fourth one said, "Let's run, let's run!"
The fifth one said, "Isn't Halloween fun?"
Then Woooooo went the wind
And OUT went the lights.
And five little pumpkins rolled out of sight.

Songs

Raffi sings "Five Little Pumpkins" on his CD *The Singable Songs Collection*. The CD *Wee Sing for Halloween* by Pamela Beall has plenty of pumpkin songs, such as "Pumpkin, Pumpkin" and "Carving Pumpkins."

Flannel-Board Rhyme

Five Little Pumpkins in a Pumpkin Patch

Five little pumpkins in a pumpkin patch sat.
Along came a ghost and took one, just like that.
Four little pumpkins by the light of the moon,
Another one was taken by a funny little goon.
Three little pumpkins in a pumpkin patch sat.
Another one was taken by a big black cat.
Two little pumpkins with little round tummies,
Another one was taken by a great big mummy.
One little pumpkin in a pumpkin patch sat.
Along came a witch and took the last one, just
   like that.
Happy Halloween!

Directions

Make five pumpkins with the pattern. To begin the rhyme, line up the five pumpkins on one side of the flannel board. Place the ghost, funny little goon, and other creatures on the opposite side of the board one by one as they are mentioned in the rhyme. Remove a pumpkin from the "pumpkin patch" and place it in each creature's hands according to the rhyme.

Craft: Peek-a-Boo Pumpkin Stick Puppet

Before the storytime, glue large orange pom-poms to craft sticks. Let dry. Provide the toddlers and caregivers with the pom-pom pumpkins and small pieces of black felt to glue on for eyes, nose, and mouth. Green felt stems could also be added. Provide paper cups that have holes poked in the bottom. Insert the bottom of the craft stick into the hole so that the pumpkin is inside the cup. Push the stick up to make the pumpkin pop out.

Supplies

Orange pom-poms
Black and green felt
Washable glue sticks
Paper cups
Craft sticks

CHAPTER 9

Let's Count

You can count on it: these stories and activities are full of numerical fun. Perform several fingerplays and count up "Five Funny Dinosaurs" on the flannel board. For the craft, show how to create a cute and colorful caterpillar made up of ten segments and a multitude of legs.

Suggested Books

Adams, Pam. *This Old Man*. Auburn, Me.: Child's Play, 2001.

Butler, John. *Ten in the Den*. Atlanta: Peachtree, 2005.

Butler, John. *Ten in the Meadow*. Atlanta: Peachtree, 2006.

Carroll, Kathleen Sullivan. *One Red Rooster*. Boston: Houghton Mifflin, 1992.

Katz, Karen. *Counting Kisses*. New York: McElderry, 2001.

Lee, Kate. *Snappy Little Numbers*. Brookfield, Conn.: Millbrook, 1998.

Miller, Virginia. *Ten Red Apples*. Cambridge, Mass.: Candlewick, 2002.

Parker, Victoria. *Bearobics: A Hip-Hop Counting Story*. New York: Viking, 1997.

Peek, Merle. *Roll Over: A Counting Song*. New York: Houghton Mifflin/Clarion, 1981.

Stickland, Paul. *Ten Terrible Dinosaurs*. New York: Dutton, 1997.

Fingerplays and Rhymes

Bouncy Ball

Here is a big round bouncy ball.
I bounce it 1, 2, 3.
Here is a ball for throwing.
I can catch it,
Watch and see.
Here is a ball for rolling.
Please roll it back to me.
Bouncing, throwing, rolling balls;
Let's count them: 1, 2, 3.

(Use a large Nerf ball to perform the actions in the rhyme. Give each toddler a turn at rolling the ball back to you.)

Catching a Fish
(Mother Goose)

One, Two, Three, Four, Five,
(count fingers on left hand)
I caught a little fish alive.
(catch fingers on right hand with left hand)
Why did you let it go?
(release fingers quickly)
Because it bit my fingers so.
(shake right hand)
Which finger did it bite?
The little finger on the right.
(point to little finger on right hand)

Songs

Ten in the Bed
(traditional song)

There were ten in the bed,
(hold up two hands, fingers extended)
And the little one said,
(wiggle a pinkie)
Roll over, roll over!
(make fists and roll arms)
So they all rolled over,
And one fell out.
There were nine in bed,
(hold up two hands, nine fingers extended)
(repeat lines until one remains)
There was one in bed,
And the little one said,
Good Night!

(Additional songs: "This Old Man," "Six Little Ducks," and "Roll Over" can be found on the CD *Toddler Tunes: 25 Classic Songs for Toddlers*. You'll find "Let's Do the Numbers Rumba" on Raffi's *Rise and Shine* CD.)

Flannel-Board Song

Five Funny Dinosaurs
(adapted from traditional song "Five Green Speckled Frogs"; see song discography)

Five funny dinosaurs
Let out a great big roar
And ate up some most delicious leaves,
Yum! Yum!
One jumped into a pool,
Where it was nice and cool.
Then there were four funny dinosaurs.
Roar, roar!
(repeat for four, three, two, one, and no funny dinosaurs)

Directions

Cut out an oval of blue felt to represent the pool. Place the dinosaurs near the pool on the flannel board. On "one jumped into the pool," place each dinosaur on the pool in turn according to the song.

Craft: Counting Caterpillar

To prepare for the craft, cut out a supply of small circles (caterpillar segments) from many different colors of construction paper. You will need ten per toddler. Let the toddlers glue the circles onto a construction-paper background to create a long, colorful caterpillar whose segments and legs are fun to count. Washable markers or crayons may be used to create a funny face, antennae, and a multitude of legs.

Supplies

Construction paper
Washable glue sticks
Washable markers or crayons

CHAPTER 10

Little, Adorable Me

In this storytime, toddlers will learn all about themselves and all the wonderful things they can do. Enjoy terrific stories and fingerplays, and give the toddlers egg shakers to shake along to songs on Hap Palmer's CD *So Big: Activity Songs for Little Ones.* Next, present a flannel-board story about a little bear who learns how to dress himself. Finally, show how to decorate a picture frame for a picture of "Little, Adorable Me."

Suggested Books

Butler, John. *Can You Cuddle Like a Koala?* Atlanta: Peachtree, 2003.

Carle, Eric. *From Head to Toe.* New York: Harper-Collins, 1997.

Carter, David. *If You're Happy and You Know It: A Pop-Up Book.* New York: Scholastic, 1997.

Cauley, Lorinda Bryan. *Clap Your Hands.* New York: Putnam, 1992.

Intrater, Roberta Grobel. *Peek-a-Boo, You!* New York: Scholastic, 2002.

Isadora, Rachel. *I Hear.* New York: Greenwillow, 1985.

Martin, Bill. *Here Are My Hands.* New York: Holt, 1985.

Martin, David. *We've All Got Bellybuttons!* Cambridge, Mass.: Candlewick, 2005.

Williams, Sue. *I Went Walking.* San Diego: Harcourt Brace, 1990.

Wood, Audrey. *Quick as a Cricket.* Singapore: Child's Play, 1982.

Fingerplays and Rhymes

Open and Shut Them
(folk rhyme; suit actions to words)

Open and shut them,
Open and shut them,
(hold hands up, palms out)
Give a little clap.
Open and shut them,
Open and shut them,
Put them in your lap.
Creep them, creep them,
Creep them, creep them,
Right up to your chin.
Open up your little mouth
But do not let them in!
(quickly put hands behind back)

We Can Jump
(folk rhyme)

We can jump, jump, jump.
We can hop, hop, hop.
We can clap, clap, clap.
We can stop, stop, stop.
We can stretch up both our arms.
We can reach and touch our toes.
We can bend our knees a little bit,
And sit down slow.

Songs

This Little Light of Mine
(traditional; see song discography for tune)

This little light of mine,
I'm gonna let it shine.
This little light of mine,
I'm gonna let it shine.
This little light of mine,
I'm gonna let it shine.
Let it shine,
Let it shine,
Let it shine.

(Additional songs: A wonderful CD with many easy to follow action songs is Hap Palmer's *So Big: Activity Songs for Little Ones*. Use egg shakers with "Rock and Roll Freeze Dance.")

Flannel-Board Story

In the story *How Do I Put It On?* by Shigeo Watanabe, a little bear shows the wrong way and the right way to put on clothing. Toddlers will enjoy telling the right way to put on the clothes.

Directions

Obtain a copy of the book and learn the story. Place the bear on the flannel board, and demonstrate the different ways that the bear tries on the items of clothing. He starts out by putting the shirt on like pants, and so on. Let the toddlers tell you the right way to put on the clothing items and then put them on the bear correctly. Make all the story figures from felt so the clothes will stick to the bear.

Craft: A Picture of Little, Adorable Me

Ask the parents and other caregivers to bring in snapshots of their toddlers. Before the program, glue wide craft sticks together to make simple picture frames. Glue heavy white paper on as a backing. Glue magnets to the back so the picture can be placed on a refrigerator. Let the toddlers, with the help of caregivers, glue their picture to the white backing. Next, the fun part, let them decorate the frames with fun craft materials such as feathers, pom-poms, stickers, or whatever else you can think of.

Supplies

Craft sticks
Heavy paper
Magnets
Washable glue sticks
Feathers
Pom-poms
Stickers

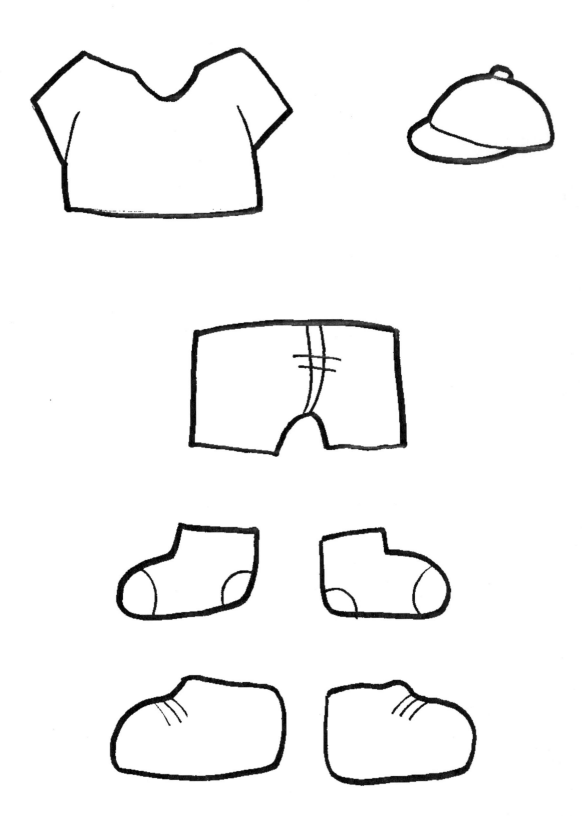

CHAPTER 11

Monkeyshines

There is plenty of monkey business going on in this storytime. Introduce the program with a monkey puppet. Have the puppet perform the actions to the rhyme "Monkey See, Monkey Do." Use the flannel board to present "Five Little Monkeys Jumping on the Bed." Show how to make a cute tube monkey.

Suggested Books

Alborough, Jez. *Hug*. Cambridge, Mass.: Candlewick, 2000.

Alborough, Jez. *Tall*. Cambridge, Mass.: Candlewick, 2005.

Bornstein, Ruth. *Little Gorilla*. New York: Houghton Mifflin, 2000.

Christelow, Eilene. *Five Little Monkeys Jumping on the Bed*. New York: Clarion, 1989.

Christelow, Eilene. *Five Little Monkeys Sitting in a Tree*. New York: Clarion, 1991.

MacKinnon, Debbie. *Meg's Monkey: A Lift-a-Flap Board Book*. New York: Dial Books for Young Readers, 1996.

Oxenbury, Helen. *Tom and Pippo on the Beach*. Cambridge, Mass.: Candlewick, 1993.

Rathmann, Peggy. *Good Night, Gorilla*. New York: Putnam, 1994.

Schindel, John. *Busy Monkeys*. Berkeley, Calif.: Tricycle, 2002.

Thompson, Kim Mitzo. *Five Little Monkeys Jumping on the Bed (Sing-a-Story)*. Columbus, Ohio: School Specialty, 2006.

Fingerplays and Rhymes

Itsy Bitsy Monkey
(folk rhyme)

The itsy bitsy monkey climbed up the coconut tree.
(hands climb)
Down came a coconut that bopped him on the knee.
(drop fist from over head to hit yourself on the knee)
Along came his Mama, who kissed away the pain,
(kiss your fist)
Then the itsy bitsy monkey climbed up the tree again.
(climb hands again, having kids stretch as high as they can reach)

Five Little Monkeys and the Crocodile
(folk rhyme)

Five little monkeys
(hold up hand to show five fingers)
Swinging in a tree,

Teasing Mr. Crocodile,
Can't catch me, can't catch me!
(shake one finger)
Along comes Crocodile,
(form crocodile jaws with hands)
Quiet as can be,
And SNAPS that monkey
(snap hands shut)
Right out of that tree!
(repeat for four, three, two, and one)
Oh, oh. No more monkeys swinging in a tree.

Monkey See, Monkey Do
(folk rhyme)
(Match actions to words)

Oh when you clap, clap, clap your hands,
The monkey claps, claps, claps his hands.
Chorus:
Monkey see, monkey do.
Monkey does the same as you!
(repeat chorus between each of the following
    verses)
Oh when you stamp, stamp, stamp your feet . . .
Oh when you jump, jump, jump up high . . .
Oh when you turn yourself around . . .

(Idea: While you lead the toddlers and caregivers
in the actions, have an assistant do the actions
with a monkey puppet.)

Songs

Pop Goes the Weasel
(see song discography for tune)

All around the mulberry bush
The monkey chased the weasel.
The monkey thought 'twas all in fun.
Pop goes the weasel.
A penny for a spool of thread,
A penny for a needle.
That's the way the money goes.
Pop goes the weasel.

(Additional songs: You'll find "Monkey See, Monkey Do" on the CD *Makin' Music: Boogie to the Beat.* "Here Sits a Monkey" is on Raffi's CD *The Corner Grocery Store.*)

Flannel-Board Rhyme

Five Little Monkeys Jumping on the Bed
(folk rhyme)

Five little monkeys jumping on the bed.
One fell off and bumped his head.
Mama called the doctor and the doctor said,
No more monkeys jumping on the bed!!
(repeat for four, three, two, one, and then give
    the last line)
Put those monkeys straight to bed!

Directions

Start the rhyme with all the monkeys except the
mother on the flannel board. Place the little monkeys above the bed as if jumping. Remove the
monkeys one by one as they fall off the bed. On
"Mama called the doctor," place the mother on the
board.

Craft: Tube Monkey

Prepare for this craft by making tubes from brown
card stock and tape. Poke holes in the tubes so
brown pipe cleaners can be attached for arms,
legs, and a curly tail. Let caregivers help the toddlers attach the pipe cleaners and glue on a face
cut out of brown construction paper, with a monkey face drawn on it in crayon or pencil.

Supplies

Brown card stock
Washable glue sticks
Brown pipe cleaners
Tape

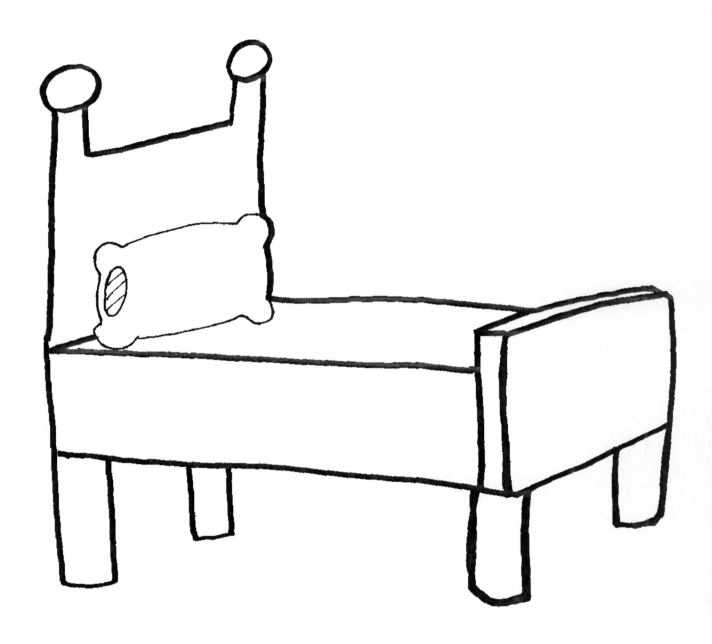

CHAPTER 12

My Daddy and I

Enjoy wonderful Daddy stories and sing Daddy songs. Present "Where's My Daddy?" on the flannel board, and show how to create a fishing pole and a fish you can catch!

Suggested Books

Bauer, Marion Dane. *The Very Best Daddy of All.* New York: Simon and Schuster, 2004.

Braun, Sebastien. *I Love My Daddy.* New York: HarperCollins, 2004.

Carle, Eric. *Papa, Please Get the Moon for Me.* New York: Simon and Schuster, 1986.

Gutman, Anne. *Daddy Cuddles.* San Francisco, Calif.: Chronicle, 2005.

Gutman, Anne. *Daddy Kisses.* San Francisco, Calif.: Chronicle, 2003.

Katz, Karen. *Daddy and Me: A Lift-a-Flap Book.* New York: Little Simon, 2003.

Katz, Karen. *Daddy Hugs 1, 2, 3.* New York: McElderry, 2005.

Porter-Gaylord, Laurel. *I Love My Daddy Because.* New York: Dutton, 1991.

Watanabe, Shigeo. *Daddy, Play with Me.* New York: Philomel, 1985.

Watanabe, Shigeo. *Where's My Daddy?* New York: Philomel, 1982.

Fingerplays and Rhymes

Here Is a Little Girl

Here is a little girl ready for her nap.
(hold up one finger)
Lay her down in her daddy's lap.
(place finger in palm)
Cover her up, so she won't peep,
(close hand over finger)
Rock her till she's fast asleep.
(rock hand back and forth)

Finger Family

This is mommy, kind and dear.
(point to thumb)
This is daddy, standing near.
(point to index finger)
This is brother, see how tall!
(point to middle finger)
This is sister, not so tall.
(point to ring finger)
This is baby, sweet and small.
(point to little finger)
They are family, one and all!
(wiggle all fingers)

Songs

Daddy-o
(tune: Bingo)

There is a great man who I love,
And Daddy is his name-o.
D-A-D-D-Y, D-A-D-D-Y, D-A-D-D-Y,
And Daddy is his name-o.
He plays with me and reads me books,
And I really love him.
D-A-D-D-Y, D-A-D-D-Y, D-A-D-D-Y,
And Daddy is his name-o.
(clap hands while spelling out daddy)

My Daddy Is Really Quite Special
(tune: "My Bonnie Lies over the Ocean")

My daddy is really quite special,
My daddy is really quite fine,
He hugs me, and helps me, and loves me,
I'm so very glad that he's mine.
Oh Daddy, Oh Daddy,
You are the greatest to me, to me!
Oh Daddy, Oh Daddy,
You are the greatest to me!

Flannel-Board Story

Where's My Daddy? by Shigeo Watanabe is the story of a little bear who, on a search for his daddy, asks several different animals if they have seen him.

Directions

Obtain a copy of the book and learn the story. Place each animal on the flannel board on cue according to the story. Remove each animal when the next animal appears. Display a copy of the book.

Craft: Fish and Pole

To prepare for the craft, cut fish shapes out of heavy paper. Let the toddlers and caregivers decorate the fish by gluing on pieces of colored tissue paper or shiny scales precut from shiny wrapping paper. Other details may be added with washable markers. Attach a large paper clip to the mouth area of the fish. Next create fishing poles with cardboard tubes. Make them about a foot long. Tie a length of yarn to the end of each pole. Attach a stick-on magnet to the end of the yarn. Now go fishing! (For additional activities with a fish and pole, see the "Go Fish" activity in chapter 4.)

Supplies

Heavy paper
Washable glue sticks
Colored tissue paper
Shiny wrapping paper
Washable markers
Paper clips
Cardboard tubes
Yarn
Stick-on magnets

CHAPTER 13

My Mommy and I

Enjoy all kinds of marvelous Mommy stories, fingerplays, and songs. Present the funny story *Mother, Mother, I Want Another* on the flannel board. Show how to create a bouquet of colorful daisies.

Suggested Books

Bauer, Marion Dane. *My Mother Is Mine.* New York: Simon and Schuster, 2001.

Braun, Sebastien. *I Love My Mommy.* New York: HarperCollins, 2004.

Brown, Margaret Wise. *The Runaway Bunny.* New York: HarperCollins, 1942.

Gutman, Anne. *Mommy Hugs.* San Francisco, Calif.: Chronicle, 2003.

Gutman, Anne. *Mommy Loves.* San Francisco, Calif.: Chronicle, 2005.

Katz, Karen. *Counting Kisses.* New York: McElderry, 2001.

Katz, Karen. *Mommy Hugs.* New York: McElderry, 2006.

Katz, Karen. *Where Is Baby's Mommy?* New York: Little Simon, 2000.

Parr, Todd. *The Mommy Book.* Boston: Little, Brown, 2002.

Porter-Gaylord, Laurel. *I Love My Mommy Because.* New York: Dutton, 1991.

Fingerplays and Rhymes

My Mommy

My Mommy is very special,
I think that you'll agree,
She picks the greatest stories
(hold palms out, pretend to read)
To read aloud to me.
Sometimes we go fishing,
(pretend to cast out line)
Or play a game of ball.
(pretend to toss a ball)
She always gives me great big hugs,
(hug Mom)
She's the best mom of them all!

I Love Mommy
(folk rhyme; tune: "Frère Jacques")

I love Mommy, I love Mommy,
Yes I do, yes I do,
Mommies are for hugging,
(hug Mom)
Mommies are for kissing,
(kiss Mom)
I love you, yes I do!

Songs

Five Little Ducks
(nursery rhyme)

Five little ducks went out one day,
Over the hills and far away.
Mother Duck cried,
"Quack, quack, quack!"
But only four little ducks
Came back.
(repeat for four, three, two, and one)
No little ducks went out to play
Over the hills and far away.
Mother Duck cried,
"Quack! Quack! Quack!"
And all the little ducks
Came running back!

Sweet, Dear Mommy
(tune: "You Are My Sunshine")

You are my Mommy,
My sweet dear Mommy,
You make me happy,
When skies are blue.
I want to tell you,
How much I love you!
You are the best mommy,
That's so true!

Flannel-Board Story

Mother, Mother, I Want Another by Maria Polushkin is the story of a young mouse who asks his mother for another kiss at bedtime but his mother doesn't quite understand what he wants.

Directions

Obtain a copy of the book and learn the story. Begin the story with the baby mouse and the mother mouse on the flannel board. Add all the other mothers in turn according to the story. Remove the mouse mother from the board briefly when she goes in search of each mother. Display a copy of the book.

Craft: Daisies for Mom

To prepare for the craft, cut out a supply of circles of all colors from construction paper. Next, cut snips all around the circles to create daisy petals, leaving the center uncut. Let the toddlers and caregivers color the centers different colors and glue the flowers onto pipe-cleaner stems. Let them make enough to form small bouquets.

Supplies

Construction paper
Washable markers
Washable glue sticks
Pipe cleaners

CHAPTER 14

Noisy Stories

Crash! Bang! Roar! Squeak! Let's make a whole lot of noise! This storytime is full of boisterous stories and uproarious fun. As for the craft, what could be more fun to listen to than the reverberation of a band of kazoos?

Suggested Books

Bryant, Lorinda Cauley. *Clap Your Hands*. New York: Putnam, 1992.

Butler, John. *Who Says Woof?* New York: Viking, 2003.

Cimarusti, Marie Torres. *Peek-a-Moo!* New York: Dutton, 1998.

Dodd, Emma. *Dog's Noisy Day*. New York: Dutton, 2003.

Martin, Bill. *Polar Bear, Polar Bear, What Do You Hear?* New York: Holt, 1991.

Matthew, Derek. *Snappy Sounds Roar!* Berkeley, Calif.: Silver Dolphin, 2004.

McGee, Marni. *The Noisy Farm*. New York: Bloomsbury Children's Books, 2004.

O'Connell, Rebecca. *The Baby Goes Beep*. Brookfield, Conn.: Roaring Brook, 2003.

Walsh, Melanie. *Do Monkeys Tweet?* Boston: Houghton Mifflin, 1997.

Weatherford, Carole Boston. *Jazz Baby*. New York: Lee and Low, 2002.

Whybrow, Ian. *The Noisy Way to Bed*. New York: Arthur A. Levine, 2004.

Wojtowycz, David. *Can You Choo Choo?* New York: Scholastic, 2003.

Wojtowycz, David. *Can You Moo?* New York: Scholastic, 2003.

Fingerplays and Rhymes

Choo-Choo Train
(folk rhyme)

Choo-choo train, choo-choo train,
(hold waist and sway)
Puffing down the track,
Now it's going forward,
(move arms bent at sides in a circular motion
and move forward)
Now it's going back.
(move arms in opposite direction and move
backward)
Now the bell is ringing, ding-ding,
(pull imaginary bell string)
Now the whistle blows, toot-toot.
(pull imaginary string with the other arm)
What a lot of noise it makes
(sway)
Everywhere it goes!

Let's Hear You Roar!

Let's hear you roar like a lion!
Let's see you jump like a frog.
Let's see you snap your jaws like a crocodile.
Let's hear you howl like a dog.
Pretend you're an elephant with a big, long
    trunk.
Pretend you're a monkey; let's see you jump,
    jump, jump.
And now you're a mouse. Just let me see
How very, very quiet you can be.

I'm a Tiger

I'm a tiger, hear me roar!
I'm a bear, hear me growl!
I'm a dog, hear me bark!
I'm a cat, hear me yowl!
I'm a mouse, hear me squeak!
That's how all the animals speak!

(Idea: Act out the story with puppets.)

Songs

You'll find "Let's Make Some Noise" on Raffi's CD
Everything Grows. Raffi sings "Wheels on the Bus"
on the *Raffi's Box of Sunshine* CD. Another noisy
song is "Had a Little Rooster" on the CD *Wiggles
N' Tunes Singin' Collection*.

Flannel-Board Story

Roar and More by Karla Kuskin is a book of short,
simple poems about wild animals and the noises
they make.

Directions

Attach a paper with all the rhymes on it to the
side of the board, out of sight, for easy reference.
Add each animal to the flannel board as you recite
the rhyme for each one. Use the elephant pattern
from the "Going to the Zoo" storytime (chapter 6).
Encourage the toddlers to make the animal
sounds. Display a copy of the book.

Craft: Cardboard Tube Kazoo

To create this kazoo, you can use toilet paper
tubes or paper towel tubes. Punch a hole near one
end of the tube with a hole-puncher. Next, cover
the end of the tube nearest to the hole with a
small square of waxed paper fastened on with a
rubber band. Make sure not to cover the hole you
punched in the tube. To decorate the kazoo, glue
on multicolor pieces of tissue paper. To play the
kazoo, hum a song into the open end. Parents and
other caregivers will need to assist the toddlers.

Supplies

Cardboard tubes (any kind)
Waxed paper
Rubber bands
Glue sticks
Multicolor pieces of tissue paper
Hole-puncher

CHAPTER 15

Nursery Rhyme Time

"Hey, diddle, diddle!" Enjoy marvelous Mother Goose rhymes and songs galore. Use puppets to act out some of the rhymes, such as "Two Little Black Birds" or "Little Miss Muffet." Present several rhymes on the flannel board, and show the toddlers and caregivers how to create Mary's little lamb.

Suggested Books

Adams, Pam. *This Old Man*. Auburn, Me.: Child's Play, 2001.

Baker, Keith. *Hickory Dickory Dock*. Orlando, Fla.: Harcourt, 2007.

Diamant-Cohen, Betsy. *Mother Goose on the Loose*. New York: Neal-Schuman, 2006.

Hale, Sarah Josepha Buell. *Mary Had a Little Lamb*. New York: Orchard, 1995.

Hey, Diddle, Diddle: A Children's Book of Nursery Rhymes. New York: Holt, 2003.

Linch, Tanya. *Three Little Kittens*. Columbus, Ohio: Gingham Dog, 2007.

My Very First Mother Goose. Cambridge, Mass.: Candlewick, 1996.

Taylor, Jane. *Twinkle, Twinkle, Little Star*. San Francisco, Calif.: Chronicle, 2001.

Fingerplays and Rhymes

Two Little Black Birds
(nursery rhyme)

Two little black birds
Sitting on a hill,
One named Jack,
(hold up right index finger)
One named Jill.
(hold up left index finger)
Fly away Jack,
(hide right hand behind back)
Fly away Jill.
(hide left hand behind back)
Come back Jack,
(bring right finger back)
Come back Jill.
(bring left finger back)
Two little black birds sitting on a hill.

(Idea: Use two bird stick puppets to act out this rhyme. Patterns may be found in *Toddler Story-time Programs* by Diane Briggs.)

Jack and Jill
(Mother Goose)

Jack and Jill
Went up the hill
To fetch a pail of water.

Jack fell down
And broke his crown
And Jill came tumbling after.
Up Jack got
And home did trot
As fast as he could caper,
Went to bed
And plastered his head
With vinegar and brown paper.

Songs

The *Mainly Mother Goose* CD by Sharon, Lois, and Bram contains over fifty nursery songs. Other great CDs are Raffi's *Quiet Time* and *Rise and Shine*, which feature a "Nursery Rhyme Medley," a "Nursery Rhyme Instrumental," and several other nursery songs.

Flannel-Board Rhymes

Little Miss Muffet
(Mother Goose)

Little Miss Muffet sat on a tuffet,
Eating her curds and whey;
Along came a spider,
Who sat down beside her
And frightened Miss Muffet away.

Humpty Dumpty
(Mother Goose)

Humpty Dumpty sat on a wall.
Humpty Dumpty had a great fall.
All the king's horses and all the king's men
Couldn't put Humpty together again!

Hey Diddle Diddle
(Mother Goose)

Hey diddle diddle
The cat and the fiddle
The cow jumped over the moon
The little dog laughed to see such a sight
And the dish ran away with the spoon.

Directions

Place each story figure on the flannel board on cue as you recite the lines.

Craft: Wooly Lamb with Clothespin Legs

Create little lambs or sheep to go with the nursery rhyme "Mary Had a Little Lamb," "Little Bo Peep," or "Baa, Baa, Black Sheep." To prepare for the craft, cut lamb or sheep silhouettes (without legs) from heavy pink paper. Let parents and other caregivers help the toddlers add clothespin legs. Clamp two clothespins onto the body where the legs should be. This will enable the sheep to stand. Next, glue cotton balls on each side of the sheep, and add details to the face with white crayons.

Supplies

Heavy pink paper
Two clothespins (with spring action) for each lamb
Washable glue sticks
Cotton balls
White crayons

Front

Reverse

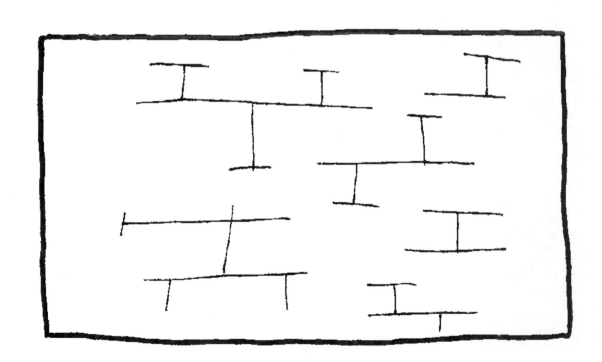

CHAPTER 16

Out Came the Sun
A Storytime about Weather

"Every cloud has a silver lining." These stories, songs, and activities feature all kinds of weather—and rainbows, too. Present the story *Rain* on the flannel board. End the program with a shiny sun mask craft.

Suggested Books

Applet, Kathi. *Rain Dance*. New York: HarperFestival, 2001.

Barry, Frances. *Duckie's Rainbow*. Cambridge, Mass.: Candlewick, 2004.

Cousins, Lucy. *Maisy's Wonderful Weather Book*. Cambridge, Mass.: Candlewick, 2006.

Greenfield, Eloise. *Water, Water*. New York: HarperFestival, 1999.

Kalan, Robert. *Rain*. New York: Greenwillow, 1978.

Ray, Mary Lyn. *Red Rubber Boot Day*. Orlando, Fla.: Harcourt, 2005.

Tafuri, Nancy. *What the Sun Sees*. New York: Greenwillow, 1997.

Fingerplays and Rhymes

Eensy, Weensy Spider
(nursery rhyme)

Eensy, weensy spider
(wiggle fingers upwards)
Climbed up the water spout.

Down came the rain
(sweep arms down and out)
And washed the spider out.
Out came the sun
(form circle over head with arms)
And dried up all the rain.
So the eensy, weensy spider
(wiggle fingers upwards)
Climbed up the spout again.

Rain

Pitter-pat, pitter-pat.
(drum fingers on the floor)
The rain goes on for hours,
And though it keeps me in the house,
It's very
(hold out two fists, palms up)
Good for
(open fists)
Flowers.
(raise and turn hands upward)

Rain on the Green Grass

Rain on the green grass,
(flutter fingers downward)
And rain on the tree,
(raise arms to indicate tree limbs)

Rain on the roof top,
(form roof above head with hands)
But not on me.
(point to self)

Songs

Mr. Sun
(traditional; see song discography for tune)

Oh Mr. Sun, Sun, Mr. Golden Sun,
Please shine down on me.
Oh Mr. Sun, Sun, Mr. Golden Sun,
Hiding behind a tree,
These little children are asking you
To please come out so we can play with you.
Oh Mr. Sun, Sun, Mr. Golden Sun,
Please shine down on,
please shine down on,
Please shine down on me.

Good Morning, Merry Sunshine
(traditional; see song discography for tune)

Good morning, Merry Sunshine,
How did you wake so soon?
You've scared the little stars away,
And shone away the moon.
I watched you go to sleep last night,
Before I stopped my play.
How did you get way over there,
And pray, where did you stay?

I never go to sleep, dear,
I just go 'round to see
My little children of the east
Who rise to watch for me.
I waken all the birds and bees
And flowers on the way,
Then last of all, the little child
Who stayed out late to play.

It's Raining, It's Pouring
(traditional; see song discography for tune)

It's raining, it's pouring,
The old man is snoring.
He went to bed and he bumped his head,
And he couldn't get up in the morning.

(Additional song: "You Are My Sunshine" can be found on the CD *Go Baby Go!* by the Baby Loves Jazz musical group.)

Flannel-Board Story

Rain by Robert Kalan contains brief text that includes a rainstorm, a rainbow, and sunshine. Many other items and their colors are featured.

Directions

Use the sun and tree patterns from "Bunnies, Eggs, and Chicks" storytime (chapter 1). Place each story figure on the board on cue as you recite the words in the book. To make rain, glue tinsel or strips of other shiny material to gray felt clouds.

Craft: Sun Mask

To prepare for the craft, cut sun shapes from card stock. Next, cut eye holes and attach a craft stick to the bottom for a holder, or let caregivers attach the sticks. Let the toddlers color their suns and glue on shiny paper, yellow feathers, and other interesting craft materials to create shiny sun masks.

Supplies

Card stock
Crayons
Shiny paper
Feathers
Glue sticks
Craft sticks

CHAPTER 17

A Rainbow of Colors

"Somewhere over the rainbow . . . " This storytime is full of vibrant stories and activities using many colors. Introduce the storytime with a colorful puppet and have it talk about the colors it's wearing, recite rhymes, or sing colorful songs. Present *Dog's Colorful Day* on the flannel board. Show how to create an adorable, multicolor Dalmatian puppy craft.

Suggested Books

Barry, Frances. *Duckie's Rainbow.* Cambridge, Mass.: Candlewick, 2004.

Cabrera, Jane. *Cat's Colors.* New York: Dial, 1997.

Cousins, Lucy. *Maisy's Rainbow Dream.* Cambridge, Mass.: Candlewick, 2003.

Dodd, Emma. *Yellow, Blue, and Bunny, Too! A Changing Picture Book of Colors.* New York: Dutton, 2001.

Fleming, Denise. *Lunch.* New York: Scholastic, 1993.

Fox, Mem. *Where Is the Green Sheep?* Orlando, Fla.: Harcourt, 2004.

Heap, Sue. *Bug in a Rug: A Lift-the-Flap Colors Book.* New York: Puffin, 2000.

Lee, Kate. *Snappy Little Colors.* San Diego, Calif.: Silver Dolphin, 2002.

Martin, Bill. *Brown Bear, Brown Bear, What Do You See?* New York: Holt, 1992.

Walsh, Ellen Stoll. *Mouse Paint.* New York: Red Wagon, 1991.

Fingerplays and Rhymes

Colors
(folk rhyme)

Blue is the sky,
(point to the sky)
Yellow is the sun,
(form circle with arms)
Silver are the moon and twinkling stars,
(make twinkling motion with fingers)
When the day is done.
(wiggle fingers in the air)
Red is the bird,
(join thumbs and flap fingers)
Green is the tree,
(raise arms over head like branches)
Brown are the chocolate cupcakes for you
    and me!
(rub tummy)

Rainbow Colors
(folk rhyme)

Rainbow purple,
(form circle with arms overhead)
Rainbow blue,

Rainbow green,
And yellow too,
Rainbow orange,
Rainbow red,
Rainbow shining over head.
Come and count
(show picture of rainbow)
The colors with me.
How many colors
Can you see?
1-2-3 on down to green,
(count on fingers)
4-5-6 colors can be seen.
Rainbow purple,
(form circle with arms overhead)
Rainbow blue,
Rainbow green,
And yellow too,
Rainbow orange,
Rainbow red,
Rainbow shining over head.

Songs

Teddy Wore His Red Shirt
(adapted from the traditional song "Mary Wore Her Red Dress"; see song discography for tune)

Teddy wore his red shirt, red shirt, red shirt,
Teddy wore his red shirt all day long.

(Continue with purple pants, white socks, blue shoes, and green hat, or use whatever colors you like. This song works very well with the flannel board. Use the patterns from *How Do I Put It On?* in chapter 10. Add the clothing pieces to the teddy bear as you sing the song.)

(Additional song: On Hap Palmer's CD *Learning Basic Skills through Music, Vol. 1*, there is a selection entitled "Colors.")

Flannel-Board Story

Dog's Colorful Day by Emma Dodd tells the story of a dog who, by the end of the day, finds himself covered with many splotches of color, such as red jam, blue paint, orange juice, and more. It all ends with a nice bath.

Directions

Obtain a copy of the book and learn the story. Make the dog figure with white felt. The spot on his ear is black. Cut out small, round pieces of felt that will be the splotches of color that get on the dog during the story. You will need the following colors: red, blue, pink, gray, orange, green, brown, yellow, and purple. As you tell the story, place the spots on the dog on cue. At the end of the story, place the dog and bathtub figure on the board. Then remove the bath figure and show the dog all clean again.

Craft: Colorful Dalmatian Puppy

This puppy will have spots that are every color of the rainbow, just like the dog in *Dog's Colorful Day*. To prepare for the craft, obtain a supply of white paper cups. Place one cup upside down. Using hot glue, or any kind of strong, quick-drying glue, attach a second cup to the bottom of the upside down cup in a horizontal position so that the second cup looks like a dog's head. The bottom or narrow end of the second cup is the snout. Let dry. Provide the toddlers and caregivers with the pre-glued cups and construction paper paws, ears, and eyes to glue on. Let them glue on pom-pom noses and multicolor spots made from construction paper or confetti.

Supplies

White paper cups (pre-glued to form a dog)
Construction paper
Washable glue sticks
Pom-poms
Confetti (optional)

CHAPTER 18

Ruff! Ruff!

"Every dog has its day." Enjoy this celebration of our canine pals. Use a dog puppet to act out rhymes and sing doggy songs. Present *The Cake That Mack Ate* on the flannel board and show how to create a paper-bag puppy.

Suggested Books

Cabrera, Jane. *Dog's Day.* New York: Orchard, 2000.

Dodd, Emma. *Dog's Colorful Day.* New York: Dutton Children's Books, 2001.

Feiffer, Jules. *Bark, George.* New York: Harper-Collins, 1999.

Harper, Isabelle. *My Dog Rosie.* New York: Blue Sky, 1994.

Hill, Eric. *Where's Spot?* New York: Putnam, 1980.

Kopper, Lisa. *Daisy's Babies.* New York: Dutton, 2000.

Pilkey, Dav. *The Complete Adventures of Big Dog and Little Dog.* New York: Harcourt, 2003.

Saltzberg, Barney. *I Love Dogs.* Cambridge, Mass.: Candlewick, 2005.

Stickland, Paul. *One Bear, One Dog.* New York: Dutton, 1997.

Stott, Dorothy. *Bingo (Sing-a-Story).* Columbus, Ohio: School Specialty, 2006.

Watt, Fiona. *That's Not My Puppy.* Tulsa, Okla.: Usborne, 2001.

Weeks, Sarah. *Ruff! Ruff! Where's Scruff?* San Diego, Calif.: Red Wagon, 2006.

Fingerplays and Rhymes

Little Puppy
(folk rhyme)

I had a little puppy,
(hold up fist)
His coat was golden brown.
One day I thought I'd bathe him,
He got dirty on the ground.
I washed my little puppy,
(scrub fist with other hand),
Then dried him with a towel.
(pat fist like drying with a towel)
My puppy seemed to like his bath,
He didn't even growl.

Digging in the Dirt
(folk rhyme)

Ten little doggies went out one day
(hold ten fingers up)
To dig in the dirt and play, play, play.
(pretend to dig like a dog with both hands)
Five were spotted, and five were not,
(hold up one hand at a time)
And at dinner time they ate a lot!
(pretend to eat)

Songs

Do Your Ears Hang Low?
(traditional; see song discography for tune)

Do your ears hang low?
Do they wobble to and fro?
Can you tie them in a knot?
Can you tie them in a bow?
Can you throw them over your shoulder
Like a continental soldier?
Do your ears hang low?

(Idea: Act out the song with a stuffed toy dog or puppet with long, floppy ears.)

Where Oh Where Has My Little Dog Gone?
(traditional; see song discography for tune)

Where oh where has my little dog gone?
Oh where oh where can he be?
With his tail cut short and his ears cut long,
Oh where oh where can he be?

(Idea: Bring a dog puppet out after you sing this song. Now have the puppet sing another dog song such as "Baby's Good Doggy" by Hap Palmer. This song can be found on the CD *Babysong*.)

My Dog Rags
(traditional; see song discography for tune)

I have a dog and his name is Rags.
He eats so much that his tummy sags!
His ears flip-flop and his tail wig-wags,
And when he walks, he walks zig-zag!
He goes flip-flop, wig-wag, zig-zag.
(sing the flip-flop line three times)
I love Rags and he loves me.

My dog Rags loves to play.
He rolls around in the mud all day.
I call, he won't obey!
He always runs the other way.
He goes flip-flop, wig-wag, zig-zag.
(sing the flip-flop line three times)
I love Rags and he loves me.

Flannel-Board Story

The Cake That Mack Ate by Rose Robart is a cumulative tale about the making of a cake. A surprise occurs when a cute pooch named Mack makes an appearance at the end of the story.

Directions

Place each story figure on the flannel board in succession according to the story. Place Mack next to the cake with his mouth on the cake at the end of the story. (Note: Another flannel-board story that will work well with this theme is "Dog's Colorful Day" in chapter 17.)

Craft: Paper-Bag Puppy

Let caregivers help the toddlers glue precut, construction-paper legs, tails, ears, eyes, and tongues onto a paper bag. Or you could let the adults cut out the pieces before gluing. Glue on a pom-pom nose and your cute puppy is done.

Supplies

Paper bags
Construction paper
Pom-poms
Washable glue sticks

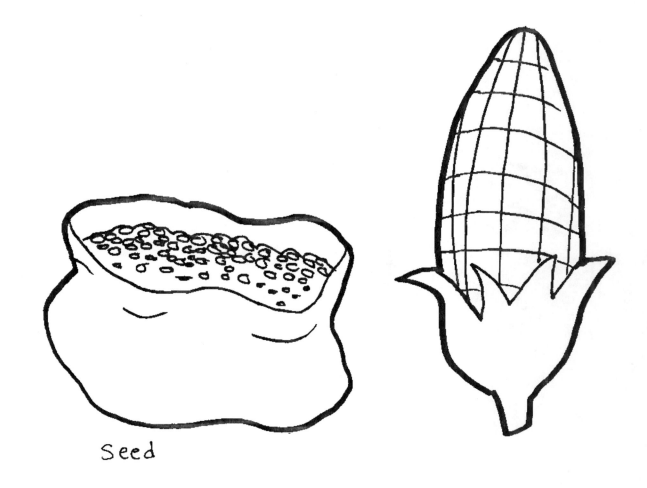

Seed

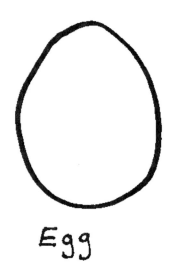

Egg

Candles

CHAPTER 19

Silly Stuff

Revel in silly stories and activities and enjoy lots of giggles, chuckles, and laughs. Pass out egg shakers and let the toddlers shake along to "Shake My Sillies Out" from Raffi's *More Singable Songs* CD. Use a clown puppet as a host and let him or her sing plenty of silly little ditties. For the craft, show how to create a silly bouncing bug.

Suggested Books

Christelow, Eilene. *Five Little Monkeys Jumping on the Bed*. New York: Clarion, 1989.

Cimarusti, Marie Torres. *Peek-a-Moo!* New York: Dutton Children's Books, 1998.

Cronin, Doreen. *Wiggle*. New York: Atheneum, 2005.

Durango, Julia. *Cha-cha Chimps*. New York: Simon and Schuster, 2006.

McDonnell, Flora. *Splash!* Cambridge, Mass.: Candlewick, 1999.

Shannon, David. *Oops!* New York: Blue Sky, 2005.

Tafuri, Nancy. *Silly Little Goose!* New York: Scholastic, 2001.

Weeks, Sarah. *Overboard!* Orlando, Fla.: Harcourt, 2006.

Wood, Audrey. *Silly Sally*. San Diego, Calif.: Harcourt Brace Jovanovich, 1991.

Yaccarino, Dan. *An Octopus Followed Me Home*. New York: Viking, 1997.

Fingerplays and Rhymes

Criss, Cross, Applesauce
(folk rhyme)

Criss, cross, applesauce
(draw an X on child's back)
Big squeeze
(hug child)
Cool breeze
(blow on back of child's neck)
Now you've got the shivers!
(tickle all over)

Five Little Monkeys
(folk rhyme)

Five little monkeys jumping on the bed,
(pretend to jump on bed)
One fell off and bumped his head.
(tap forehead with fingers)
Mama called the doctor and the doctor said,
(pretend to dial phone)
No more monkeys jumping on the bed!!
(shake index finger)
(repeat for four, three, two, and one, then give the last line)
Put those monkeys straight to bed!

Songs

Head, Shoulders, Knees, and Toes
(traditional action song)

Head, shoulders, knees, and toes,
Knees and toes.
Head, shoulders, knees, and toes,
Knees and toes.
Eyes and ears and mouth and nose
Head, shoulders, knees, and toes
(touch the places on your body as you sing)

(Additional songs: Give the toddlers egg shakers and let them shake along to "Shake My Sillies Out" from Raffi's *More Singable Songs* CD. You'll find more great silly songs on the CD *Silly Favorites* from Music for Little People.)

Flannel-Board Stories

Several flannel-board stories in this book will work well with this theme. Add any one or all of these to your storytime: "How Do I Put It On?" in chapter 10, "Five Little Monkeys Jumping on the Bed" in chapter 11, or "A Kiss for Little Bear" in chapter 21.

Craft: Silly Bouncing Bug

To prepare for the craft session, first form the poles from which the silly bugs will dangle. For each toddler, attach a piece of elastic string to a sturdy plastic straw. Glue a large pom-pom to the other end of the elastic string. At the craft session, provide the toddlers and caregivers with funny stuff to glue onto the pom-poms, such as paper legs, feathers, little pieces of fake fur, and funny paper eyes.

Supplies

Sturdy plastic straws
Elastic string
Pom-poms
Glue sticks
Construction-paper cut-outs of legs, eyes, and so on
Feathers
Small pieces of fake fur

CHAPTER 20

Squeak and Meow

These stories are filled with cool cats and marvelous mice. Introduce the storytime with puppets of a cat and a mouse. Using the puppets, perform the nursery rhyme "Pussy Cat, Pussy Cat." Next, have the cat puppet sing "Kitty Diddy, Diddy Dum Diddy Do." Present the hungry mouse story *Lunch* on the flannel board. For more fun, show how to create a cute egg-carton mouse.

Suggested Books

Baker, Keith. *Hickory Dickory Dock*. Orlando, Fla.: Harcourt, 2007.

Bogacki, Tomek. *Cat and Mouse in the Snow*. New York: Farrar, Straus and Giroux, 1999.

Bogacki, Tomek. *Cat and Mouse*. New York: Farrar, Straus and Giroux. 1996.

Cabrera, Jane. *Cat's Colors*. New York: Dial Books for Young Readers, 1997.

Casey, Patricia. *My Cat Jack*. London: Walker, 2004.

Fleming, Denise. *Lunch*. New York: Holt, 1993.

Riley, Linnea. *Mouse Mess*. New York: Blue Sky, 1997.

Watt, Fiona. *That's Not My Kitten*. Tulsa, Okla.: EDC Publishers, 2001.

Wilson, Karma. *Hello, Calico!* New York: Little Simon, 2007.

Wood, Don. *The Little Mouse, the Red Ripe Strawberry, and the Big Hungry Bear*. New York: Scholastic, 1994.

Yolen, Jane *Mouse's Birthday*. New York: Putnam, 1993.

Fingerplays and Rhymes

Little Mousie
(folk rhyme)

Here's a little mousie,
Peeking through a hole.
(poke index finger through fist of the other hand)
Peek to the left,
(wiggle finger to the left)
Peek to the right.
(wiggle finger to the right)
Pull your head back in,
(pull finger into fist)
There's a cat in sight!

Little Kittens
(folk rhyme)

Five little kittens
(hand made into a fist)
All fluffy and white
Sleeping and purring

111

All through the night.
It's time to get up now, sleepy heads.
Meow, meow, meow, meow, meow,
(each finger raised in turn to "Meow")
Five little kittens all up from their beds.

Pussycat, Pussycat
(nursery rhyme)

Pussycat, pussycat, where have you been?
I've been to London to visit the Queen.
Pussycat, pussycat, what did you there?
I frightened a little mouse under her chair.
(act out with puppets)

Songs

Kitty Diddy, Diddy Dum Diddy Do
(tune: "Do Wah Diddy")

Here she comes, just a padding down the street,
Singing "Kitty diddy, diddy dum diddy do."
Watch out little mousey, she's hungry and wants
    to eat,
Yowling "Kitty diddy, diddy dum diddy do."
She's soft. She's soft. But she's strong. She's
    strong.
She's soft, she's strong, won't be hungry very
    long.
Kitty diddy, diddy dum diddy do.

(Idea: Use a cat puppet to sing this song.)

(Additional songs: On the *Mainly Mother Goose* CD by Sharon, Lois, and Bram, you'll find cat and mouse songs such as "Three Little Kittens," "Pussy Cat, Pussy Cat," "Hickory, Dickory, Dock," and "Three Blind Mice.")

Flannel-Board Story

Lunch by Denise Fleming is the story of a very hungry mouse that devours a giant lunch made up of colorful foods.

Directions

Obtain a copy of the book and learn the story. Place the mouse and each food item on the flannel board in turn according to the story. Display a copy of the book.

Craft: Egg-Carton Mouse

To prepare for the craft, cut egg cups from egg cartons and poke a hole in the back of each. Cut out construction-paper ears. Let the toddlers and caregivers insert pipe-cleaner tails through the holes. Next, glue on pom-pom noses and the construction-paper ears. Create eyes and whiskers with washable markers.

Supplies

Egg cartons
Pipe cleaners
Pom-poms
Washable glue sticks
Construction paper
Washable markers

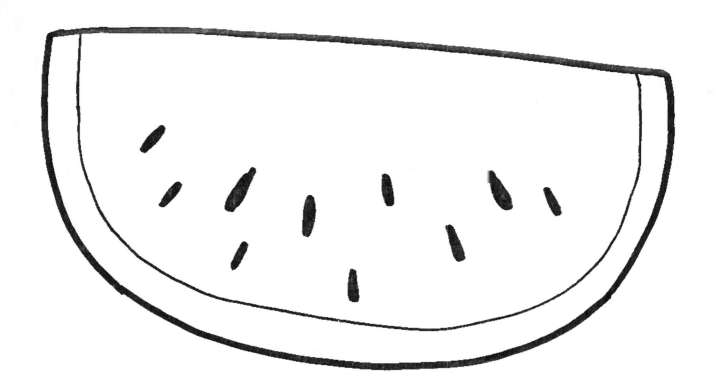

CHAPTER 21

Teddy Bear Dance

"Teddy Bear, Teddy Bear, turn around." There are bears of all kinds in these stories. Invite the toddlers to bring along a favorite bear. Introduce the program with a bear puppet and have him or her sing one or more of the bear songs suggested. On Hap Palmer's CD *So Big: Activity Songs for Little Ones*, you will find a song called "Teddy Bear Playtime." Lead the toddlers and caregivers in performing the actions in the song with a teddy bear. Present the funny story *A Kiss for Little Bear* on the flannel board. Have even more fun creating a paper-bag teddy craft.

Suggested Books

Anholt, Catherine. *Bear and Baby*. Cambridge, Mass.: Candlewick, 1993.

Blackstone, Stella. *Bear at Home*. New York: Barefoot, 2001.

Carlstrom, Nancy White. *Jesse Bear, What Will You Wear?* New York: Collier Macmillan, 1986.

Dann, Penny. *Teddy Bear, Teddy Bear, Turn Around*. Hauppauge, N.Y.: Barron's Educational Series, 2001.

Genechten, Guido van. *Because I Love You So Much*. Wilton, Conn.: Tiger Tales, 2004.

Miller, Virginia. *I Love You Just the Way You Are*. Cambridge, Mass.: Candlewick, 1998.

Parker, Victoria. *Bearobics: A Hip-Hop Counting Story*. New York: Viking, 1997.

Scott, Steve. *Teddy Bear, Teddy Bear*. New York: HarperFestival, 1998.

Stickland, Paul. *One Bear, One Dog*. New York: Dutton, 1997.

Watt, Fiona. *That's Not My Teddy*. Tulsa, Okla.: Usborne, 2000.

Wilson, Karma. *Bear Snores On*. New York: McElderry, 2002.

Wilson, Karma. *Bear Wants More*. New York: McElderry, 2003.

Wilson, Karma. *Bear's New Friend*. New York: McElderry, 2006.

Fingerplays and Rhymes

Teddy Bear, Teddy Bear
(folk rhyme)

Teddy Bear, Teddy Bear, turn around.
(match action to words in each line)
Teddy Bear, Teddy Bear, touch the ground.
Teddy Bear, Teddy Bear, dance on your toes.
Teddy Bear, Teddy Bear, touch your nose.
Teddy Bear, Teddy Bear, climb the stairs.
Teddy Bear, Teddy Bear, say your prayers.
Teddy Bear, Teddy Bear, turn out the light.
Teddy Bear, Teddy Bear, say good night.

Teddy Bear Dance

Dance with your teddy upon your toes,
(match action to words in each line)
Swing your little teddy, there he goes,
Hug your little teddy, hold him tight,
Kiss your little teddy and say goodnight.

Bear in a Cave
(folk rhyme)

Here is a cave.
(bend fingers to form cave)
Inside is a bear.
(put thumb inside fingers)
Now he comes out,
(thumb out)
To get some fresh air.
He stays out all summer
In sunshine and heat.
He hunts in the forest
(move thumb in a circle)
For berries to eat.
When snow starts to fall,
He hurries inside
His warm little cave,
(thumb in)
And there he will hide.
Snow covers the cave
Like a fluffy white rug.
(cover with other hand)
Inside the bear sleeps,
All cozy and snug.

Songs

You'll find an abundance of bear songs, such as "Teddy Bears' Picnic" and "Me and My Teddy Bear," on the *Teddy Bear Tunes* CD from Kimbo Educational. In addition, "The Bear Went over the Mountain" is on the *101 Toddler Favorites* CD from Music for Little People. "Teddy Bear Hug" is on Raffi's *Everything Grows* CD. Another great song is "Teddy Bear Playtime," which can be found on Hap Palmer's CD *So Big: Activity Songs for Little Ones*. You can also use "Teddy Wore His Red Shirt" as described in chapter 17.

Flannel-Board Story

A Kiss for Little Bear by Else Holmelund Minarik tells the story of a grandma's thank-you kiss that gets passed from animal to animal before it gets to Little Bear. A skunk's romance is helped on the way.

Directions

Obtain a copy of the book and learn the story. Place each animal on the flannel board, and remove them on cue according to the story. To indicate a kiss, place the animals nose to nose. When the skunks get married, place the veil on the girl skunk and the top hat on the boy skunk. Place all the animals on the board at the end of the story. Display a copy of the book.

Craft: Paper-Bag Teddy Bears

To prepare for the craft session, loosely stuff lunch bags with shredded paper, and tape them closed. At the craft session, ask caregivers to tie ribbons around the bags to form necks. Let the caregivers help the toddlers glue on paper ears, eyes, mouth, paws, and a pom-pom nose. Use markers to add any other details.

Supplies

Paper lunch bags
Shredded paper
Tape
Glue sticks
Ribbons
Construction paper
Pom-poms
Washable markers

CHAPTER 22

Turtles and Frogs

Splish, splash, ribbet! Enjoy terrific stories about our pond-dwelling friends. Introduce the stories with a frog puppet. Have the frog perform the rhyme "Little Frog" and sing one or more frog songs. Use a turtle puppet to act out "There Was a Little Turtle." Next, present *Jump, Frog, Jump!* on the flannel board. For the craft, show how to make a cute, colorful turtle.

Suggested Books

Falwell, Cathryn. *Turtle Splash! Countdown at the Pond.* New York: Greenwillow, 2001.

Faulkner, Keith. *The Wide-Mouthed Frog: A Pop-Up Book.* New York: Dial, 1996.

Florian, Douglas. *Turtle Day.* New York: Crowell, 1989.

Kalan, Robert. *Jump, Frog, Jump!* New York: Greenwillow, 1981.

Kelly, Martin. *Five Green and Speckled Frogs.* New York: Handprint, 2000.

Thompson, Lauren. *Little Quack's New Friend.* New York: Simon and Schuster, 2006.

Waddell, Martin. *Hi, Harry!* Cambridge, Mass.: Candlewick, 2003.

Yolen, Jane. *Dimity Duck.* New York: Philomel, 2006.

Fingerplays and Rhymes

There Was a Little Turtle
(by Vachel Lindsay)

There was a little turtle,
(make a small circle with your hands)
He lived in a box,
(make a box with both hands)
He swam in a puddle,
(wiggle hands)
He climbed on the rocks.
(climb fingers of one hand up over the other)
He snapped at a mosquito,
(clap hands)
He snapped at a flea,
(clap hands)
He snapped at a minnow,
(clap hands)
He snapped at me.
(point to yourself)
He caught the mosquito,
(mimic catching a bug)
He caught the flea,
(same action)
He caught the minnow,
(same action)
But he didn't catch me!
(point to yourself)

(Puppet idea: Perform this rhyme with a turtle puppet.)

Little Frog

I'm a little frog,
Sitting on a log.
I sing all the day long.
I have a lot to say.
Sing with me, okay?
Ribbet, ribbet, ribbet, ribbet, ribbet.

(Puppet idea: Perform this rhyme with a frog puppet.)

Five Little Green Frogs
(adapted folk rhyme)

Five little, green frogs swimming wild and free,
(perform swimming motions)
Teasing Mr. Crocodile: "You can't catch me!"
(wag index finger)
Along comes Crocodile quiet as can be.
(palms together, make a wavy motion)
And SNAP!
(snap palms together)
Four little, green frogs swimming wild and free.
(repeat until no frogs are left)

Songs

Five Green Speckled Frogs
(traditional; see song discography for tune)

Five green and speckled frogs
Sat on a speckled log,
Eating some most delicious bugs, yum-yum!
(rub tummy)
One jumped into the pool,
Where it was nice and cool,
And then there were four green speckled frogs.
Glub, glub.
(repeat until no frogs are left)

(Additional songs: You'll find the song "Tiny Tim the Turtle" on the CD *Dr. Jean Sings Silly Songs* by Jean Feldman. "The Little Turtle" is on the CD *A Twinkle in Your Eye* by Burl Ives. More frog songs, such as "Frog Went a-Courting" and "A-Goong Went the Little Green Frog," are on the CD *Sing-a-longs for Kids, Vol. 1*, from Time-Life Music.)

Flannel-Board Story

A cumulative tale, *Jump, Frog, Jump!* by Robert Kalan is the story of a frog that gets out of many tough situations by using his jumping skills.

Directions

Obtain a copy of the book and learn the story. Place each figure on the board in succession according to the story. When the frog jumps in the story, move him to another spot on the board, and remove each creature that fails to catch him. Display a copy of the book.

Craft: Colorful Paper-Bowl Turtle

To prepare for the craft session, cut turtle legs, tails, and heads out of construction paper. Let each toddler, with the help of a caregiver, glue cut-out legs, tail, and head to the rim of a paper bowl. To add color to the shell, glue on small pieces of colored tissue paper. Add details with markers.

Supplies

Construction paper
Paper bowls
Washable glue sticks
Colored tissue paper (various colors)
Washable markers

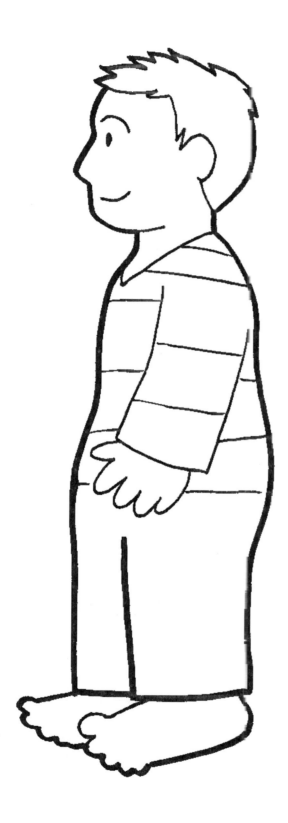

bas Ket

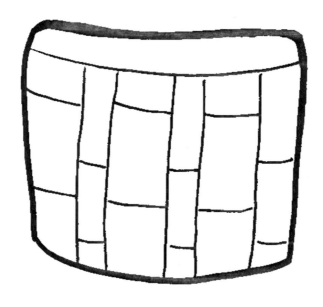

CHAPTER 23

Vroom! Zoom! Things That Go

Vroom! Vroom! Start your engines! This storytime will take you away. Introduce the program with a puppet that is dressed like a train engineer. Have him or her sing "Down by the Station" and then read a train story. Enjoy performing fingerplays about planes, trains, and automobiles. If you want even more fun, show how to make a little circus train.

Suggested Books

Barton, Byron. *My Car*. New York: Greenwillow, 2001.

Hort, Lenny. *Seals on the Bus*. New York: Holt, 2000.

Lewis, Kevin. *Chugga-Chugga Choo-Choo*. New York: Hyperion, 1999.

Lewis, Kevin. *Tugga Tugga Tugboat*. New York: Hyperion, 2006.

Sis, Peter. *Fire Truck*. New York: Greenwillow, 1998.

Spence, Robert. *Clickety Clack*. New York: Viking, 1999.

Stickland, Paul. *Truck Jam!* New York: Ragged Bears, 2000.

Sturges, Philemon. *I Love Trains*. New York: HarperFestival, 2006.

Timmers, Leo. *Who Is Driving?* New York: Bloomsbury, 2007.

Wojtowycz, David. *Can You Choo Choo?* New York: Scholastic, 2003.

Fingerplays and Rhymes

Trains, Planes, and Automobiles

Chugga, chugga, chugga like a choo-choo train.
  (match actions to words in each line)

Vroom, vroom, vroom like a car.
Zoom, zoom, zoom like an airplane.
Now come in for a landing—don't go far.

I'm a Little Truck

I'm a little truck,
Shiny and yellow.
When I go out driving,
(pretend to drive)
I'm a very happy fellow.
When the rain comes down,
(flutter fingers downward)
I turn my wipers on.
(move arms back and forth)
It's fun to splash through puddles,
All around the town.
When I see a red light.
I stop on a dime.
(stop pretending to drive)
When I see a green light,

I know it's driving time.
(pretend to drive)
Vroom! Vroom! Beep! Beep!

Airplanes

Way, way up in the sky
(raise arms high)
There is an airplane.
(point at sky)
This is how they glide.
(glide around the room)
Way, way up high,
Airplanes fly, fly, fly!

Choo-Choo Train
(folk rhyme)

Choo-choo train, choo-choo train,
(hold waist and sway)
Puffing down the track.
Now it's going forward,
(move arms bent at sides in a circular motion
    and move forward)
Now it's going back.
(move arms in opposite direction and move
    backward)
Now the bell is ringing, ding-ding,
(pull imaginary bell string)
Now the whistle blows, toot-toot.
(pull imaginary string with the other arm)
What a lot of noise it makes
(sway)
Everywhere it goes!

Songs

Down by the Station
(traditional; see song discography for tune)

Down at the station, early in the morning,
See the little Puffer Bellies all in a row.
See the engine driver pull the little handle,
Chug, chug, toot, toot,
Off they go.

(Additional songs: You'll find "Bumping Up and Down," on Raffi's CD *Singable Songs Collection* and "Riding in an Airplane" on his *One Light, One Sun.* "Wheels on the Bus" can be found on Raffi's *Rise and Shine* CD.)

Flannel-Board Story

Freight Train by Donald Crews is the story of the journey of a colorful train through tunnels, cities, and the countryside.

Directions

Obtain a copy of the book and learn the story. Place the engine and all the different colored cars on the flannel board in succession according to the story. Describe what each car is as you place it on the board.

Craft: Circus Train

To prepare for the craft session, acquire a supply of small boxes such as pint-sized milk cartons. Cut the tops off the cartons and wash them. Next, poke holes in the boxes and connect them with string to form little trains. Cut out pictures of train engines and box cars. At the craft session, provide the toddlers and their caregivers with three connected cartons each and the cut-outs of train engine and box cars to paste on the sides of the boxes. Put animal crackers in the box cars.

Supplies

Small boxes or cartons
String
Train cut-outs
Washable glue sticks
Animal crackers

CHAPTER 24

What'll We Do with the Baby-O?

Little bundles of joy abound in these stories. Enjoy fingerplays and songs all about babies, and enjoy presenting *The Elephant and the Bad Baby* on the flannel board. Show the toddlers and caregivers how to create a simple craft with hand tracings.

Suggested Books

Ashman, Linda. *Babies on the Go.* San Diego, Calif.: Harcourt, 2003.

Beaumont, Karen. *Baby Danced the Polka.* New York: Dial, 2004.

Butler, John. *Whose Baby Am I?* New York: Viking, 2001.

Cowell, Cressida. *What Shall We Do with the Boo-Hoo Baby?* New York: Scholastic, 2000.

Fleming, Candace. *This Is the Baby.* New York: Melanie Kroupa, 2004.

Katz, Karen. *Peek-a-Baby: A Lift-a-Flap Book.* New York: Little Simon, 2007.

Katz, Karen. *What Does Baby Say?* New York: Little Simon, 2004.

Katz, Karen. *Where Is Baby's Belly Button?* New York: Little Simon, 2000.

Lawrence, Michael. *Baby Loves.* New York: DK Publishing, 1999.

O'Connell, Rebecca. *The Baby Goes Beep.* Brookfield, Conn.: Roaring Brook, 2003.

Watt, Fiona. *Cuddly Baby.* Tulsa, Okla.: Usborne, 2006.

Fingerplays and Rhymes

Pat-a-Cake
(nursery rhyme)

Pat-a-cake, pat-a-cake,
Baker's man,
Bake me a cake
As fast as you can.
(clap hands rhythmically)
Roll it and pat it
(roll arms and clap hands)
And mark it with a B
(trace B on palm)
And put it in the oven
(pretend to put in oven)
For baby and me.
(point to baby and self)

Baby's Nap
(folk rhyme)

This is a baby ready for a nap.
(hold up index finger)
Lay him down in his mother's lap.
(place index finger on open palm of other hand)
Cover him up so he won't peep.

(wrap fingers around index finger)
Rock him till he's fast asleep.
(rock hands back and forth)

All for Baby
(folk rhyme)

Here's a ball for baby,
(touch fingertips of both hands together to make
    a ball)
Big and soft and round.
Here's the baby's hammer,
(pound one fist on the other)
Oh, see how he can pound.
Here is the baby's music,
(clap hands)
Clapping, clapping so,
Here are the baby's soldiers,
(hold up hands with ten fingers)
Standing in a row.
Here is baby's trumpet,
(hold one fist over the other in front of mouth)
Toot, too, too, too, too.
Here's the way that baby plays at peek-a-boo.
(cover eyes with hands)
Here's a big umbrella
(form fist with one hand and extend index finger;
    cup other hand over the finger to form an
    umbrella)
To keep the baby dry.
Here is baby's cradle,
(interlock fingers to make cradle)
Rock-a-baby bye.

One Little Baby
(folk rhyme)

One little baby rocking in the tree.
Two little babies splashing in the sea.
Three little babies crawling on the floor.
Four little babies knocking on the door.
Five little babies playing hide and seek.
Close your eyes tightly till I say "Peek!"

Songs

What'll I Do with the Baby-O?
(see song discography for tune)

What'll I do with the baby-o?
What'll I do with the baby-o?
What'll I do with the baby-o?
If he doesn't go to sleepy-o?
Wrap him up in calico,
Wrap him up in calico,
Wrap him up in calico,
Send him to his mommy-o.

Hush Little Baby
(traditional; see song discography for tune)

Hush, little baby, don't say a word,
Mama's going to buy you a mockingbird.
And if that mockingbird don't sing,
Mama's going to buy you a diamond ring.
And if that diamond ring turns brass,
Mama's going to buy you a looking-glass.
And if that looking-glass gets broke,
Mama's going to buy you a billy goat.
And if that billy goat won't pull,
Mama's going to buy you a cart and bull.
And if that cart and bull turn over,
Mama's going to buy you a dog named Rover.
And if that dog named Rover won't bark,
Mama's going to buy you a horse and cart.
And if that horse and cart fall down,
You'll still be the sweetest little baby in town.

(Additional songs: On the CD *Baby-O!* by MaryLee
Sunseri, you'll find more baby themed songs such
as "Peek-a-Boo" and "Here's a Ball for Baby.")

Flannel-Board Story

The Elephant and the Bad Baby by Elfrida Vipont
is a story about a baby who gets anything he
wants from his elephant friend as he rides around
town on the elephant's back. Each time the baby
receives another treat, they continue "rumpeta,
rumpeta, rumpeta, all down the road" with more
and more people chasing after them.

Directions

Obtain a copy of the book and learn the story. On the flannel board, place the baby on the elephant's back. As you tell the story, put the food items that are filched from the various stores on the elephant's back next to the baby. Add the townspeople to the board on cue as they appear in the story. Position them so they look like they are chasing the elephant. At the end of the story, put the mother with the pancakes on the board. To end the story, remove the elephant and each townsperson in succession and place the baby on the bed.

Craft: Cut-out Flowers

Have the caregivers trace their toddler's hands and their own on paper and then cut out the hand shapes. Ask the caregivers to cut out several sets of the hands using the original tracing. Use a variety of colored paper. Using glue sticks, caregivers can help the toddlers paste the hands onto construction paper in a flower shape. Provide pre-cut stems and leaves to paste on beneath the flower shape, or let the caregivers cut out stems and leaves.

Supplies

Paper in various colors
Construction paper
Pencils
Glue sticks
Scissors

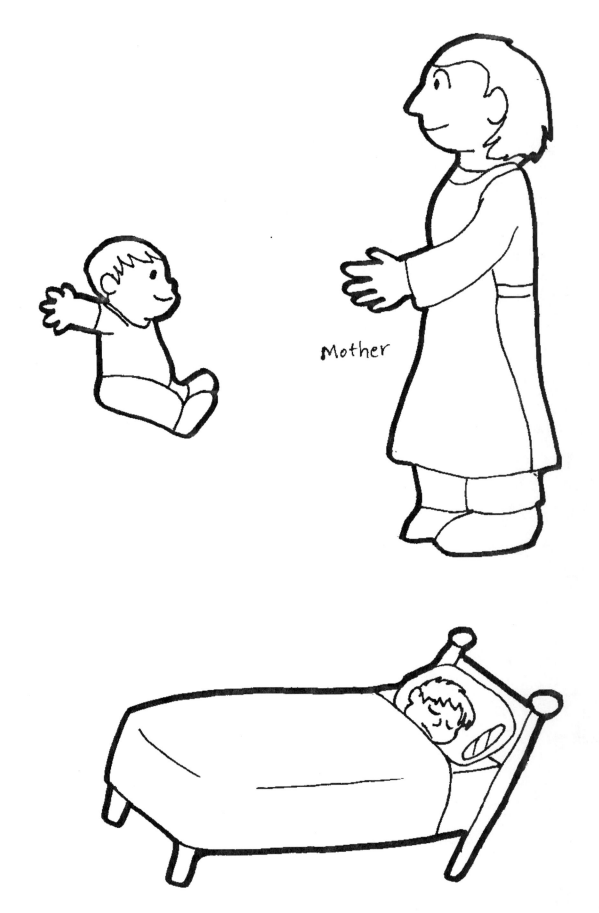

Mother

Grocer

Candy shop
lady

Butcher

Baker

fruit & Vegetable man

ice cream man

snack Shop man

CHAPTER 25

Yummers

Enjoy a feast of yummy tales, fingerplays, and activities. Have a puppet host sing several of the delicious songs suggested. Present tasty rhymes and stories on the flannel board. To end the program, show how to decorate delectable cookies.

Suggested Books

Carle, Eric. *The Very Hungry Caterpillar*. New York: Philomel, 1969.

Degen, Bruce. *Jamberry*. New York: Harper and Row, 1983.

Dunrea, Olivier. *BooBoo*. Boston: Houghton Mifflin, 2004.

Falwell, Cathryn. *Feast for 10*. New York: Houghton Mifflin, 1996.

Fleming, Denise. *Lunch*. New York: Holt, 1993.

Hill, Eric. *Spot Bakes a Cake*. New York: Putnam, 1994.

Numeroff, Laura. *If You Give a Mouse a Cookie*. New York: Harper and Row, 1985.

Robart, Rose. *The Cake That Mack Ate*. Boston: Little, Brown, 1986.

Van Laan, Nancy. *Tickle Tum!* New York: Atheneum, 2001.

Watanabe, Shigeo. *What a Good Lunch!* New York: Philomel, 1980.

Fingerplays and Rhymes

Hot Cross Buns
(nursery rhyme)

Hot cross buns,
(clap hands in rhythm)
Hot cross buns,
One a-penny, two a-penny.
(count out two fingers)
Hot cross buns.
(clap hands)

Pat-a-Cake
(nursery rhyme)

Pat-a-cake, pat-a-cake,
Baker's man,
Bake me a cake
As fast as you can.
(clap hands rhythmically)
Roll it and pat it
(roll arms and clap hands)
And mark it with a B
(trace B on palm)
And put it in the oven
(pretend to put in oven)
For baby and me.
(point to baby and self)

I'm a Little Teapot
(traditional)

I'm a little teapot, short and stout,
Here is my handle,
(put one hand on hip)
Here is my spout.
(extend other arm out sideways)
When I get all steamed up, and I shout,
Just tip me over and pour me out.
(bend body toward extended arm)

Songs

The CD *Songs for Wiggleworms* has several yummy songs, such as "If All of the Raindrops," "Peanut Butter and Jelly," and "Milkshake Song." You'll find "Who Stole the Cookies?" on the CD *Silly Favorites* from Music for Little People.

Flannel-Board Rhymes

Five Little Cookies
(traditional; adapt to tell of a girl or boy)

Five little cookies in a baker's shop,
Round and fat with sprinkles on top.
Along came a boy with a penny one day,
Bought a cookie and took it away.
(repeat for four, three, two, and one little
    cookie)
No little cookies in the bakery shop,
And all the cookie eating there did stop!

Directions

Place all five cookies on the flannel board. On "along came a boy (or girl)," place the boy or girl figure on the board. On "took it away," remove the child and one cookie each time until all the cookies are gone.

Five Little Ice Creams

Five little ice creams all in a row,
This one fell on a little girl's toe.
Four little ice creams yummy to see,
A little boy ate one and then there were three.
Three little ice creams all for you,
One melted away now there are two.
Two little ice creams, Oh, what fun!
My little puppy ate one and then there was one.
One little ice cream when the day is done,
We shared it together and then there was none.

Directions

Place five ice cream cones on the flannel board. Remove them one by one according to the rhyme.

Note: Two other flannel-board stories that will work well with the "Yummers" theme are *The Cake That Mack Ate* in chapter 18 and *Lunch* in chapter 20.

Craft: Decorate Cookies

In this craft, caregivers help toddlers decorate plain sugar cookies with frosting, sprinkles, and chocolate chips. Provide the caregivers and toddlers with cookies, small bowls of frosting, and decorations. Craft sticks may be used to spread the frosting.

Supplies

Sugar cookies
Frosting
Sprinkles
Chocolate chips
Craft sticks

Song Discography

"A-Goong Went the Little Green Frog." *Sing-a-longs for Kids*. New York: Time-Life Music, 2000.

"All You Need Is Love." *All You Need Is Love*. Redway, Calif.: Music for Little People, Distributed by Kid Rhino, 1999.

"At the Zoo." *Wee Sing Animals, Animals, Animals*. Pamela Beall. New York: Price Stern Sloan, 1999.

"Baa, Baa, Black Sheep." *Cheerful Baby*. Alpharetta, Ga.: Brainy Baby, 2006.

"Baby Beluga." *Raffi on Broadway*. Raffi. Universal City, Calif.: Shoreline/MCA, 1993.

"Baby Chickie." *So Big: Activity Songs for Little Ones*. Hap Palmer. Topanga, Calif.: Hap-Pal Music, 1994.

"Baby's Good Doggy." *Babysong*. Hap Palmer. Freeport, N.Y.: Activity Records, 1991.

"The Bear Went over the Mountain." *101 Toddler Favorites*. Redway, Calif.: Music for Little People, 2003.

"Bingo." *101 Toddler Favorites*. Redway, Calif.: Music for Little People, 2003.

"Bluebird." *Bottle of Sunshine*. Milkshake. Baltimore: Milkshake Music, 2004.

"Bumping Up and Down." *Singable Songs for the Very Young*. Raffi. Universal City, Calif.: Shoreline, 1976.

"Carving Pumpkins." *Wee Sing for Halloween*. Pamela Beall. New York: Price Stern Sloan, 2000.

"Colors." *Learning Basic Skills through Music, Vol. 1*. Hap Palmer. Freeport, N.Y.: Activity Records 1994.

"Do Wah Diddy." *21 Really Cool Songs: Fresh Versions of Classic Rock 'n Roll for Kids*. Sugar Beats (Musical Group). New York: Sugar Beats, 1993.

"Do Your Ears Hang Low?" *101 Toddler Favorites*. Redway Calif.: Music for Little People, 2003.

"Down by the Station." *101 Toddler Favorites*. Redway Calif.: Music for Little People, 2003.

"Down on Grandpa's Farm." *One Light, One Sun*. Raffi. Cambridge, Mass.: Rounder Records, 1985.

"Ducks Like Rain." *Rise and Shine*. Raffi. Cambridge, Mass.: Rounder Records, 1996.

"Five Green Speckled Frogs." *Five Little Monkeys*. Long Branch, N.J.: Kimbo Educational, 1999.

"Five Little Ducks." *101 Toddler Favorites*. Redway, Calif.: Music for Little People, 2003.

"Five Little Pumpkins." *Singable Songs Collection*. Raffi. Cambridge, Mass.: Rounder Records, 1996.

"Frère Jacques." *101 Toddler Favorites*. Redway, Calif.: Music for Little People, 2003.

"Frog Went a-Courting." *Sing-a-Longs for Kids, Vol. 1*. New York: Time-Life Music, 2000.

"Funny Little Bunny." *Happy Easter Songs*. New York: Sony Music, 1996.

"Going to the Zoo." *Peter, Paul, and Mommy*. Peter, Paul, and Mary. Burbank, Calif.: Warner Bros. Records, 1990.

"Good Morning, Merry Sunshine." *Patriotic and Morning Time Songs*. Hap Palmer. Freeport, N.Y.: Activity Records, 1974.

"Goodbye Song." *Songs from Jim Henson's Bear in the Big Blue House*. Burbank, Calif.: Walt Disney Records, 2000.

"Had a Little Rooster." *Wiggles N' Tunes Singin' Collection*. New York: Wiggles N' Tunes, 2002.

Happy Easter Songs. New York: Sony Music, 1996.

"Head, Shoulders, Knees, and Toes." *101 Toddler Favorites*. Redway, Calif.: Music for Little People, 2003.

"Here Sits a Monkey" *The Corner Grocery Store*. Raffi. Cambridge, Mass.: Rounder Records, 1991.

"Here's a Ball for Baby." *Baby-O!* MaryLee Sunseri. Pacific Grove, Calif.: Piper Grove Music, 2005.

"Hey, Diddle Diddle." *Three Silly Little Kittens*. Long Branch, N.J.: Kimbo Educational, 2002.

"Hickory, Dickory, Dock." *Mainly Mother Goose*. Sharon, Lois, and Bram. Toronto: Elephant Records; Los Angeles: Drive Entertainment, 1994.

"Hush, Little Baby." *101 Toddler Favorites*. Redway, Calif.: Music for Little People, 2003.

"If All of the Raindrops." *Songs for Wiggleworms*. Chicago: Old Town School of Folk Music, 2000.

"It's Raining, It's Pouring." *Preschool Songs: 15 Fun Songs for Kids*. Nashville, Tenn.: Word Entertainment, Warner/Curb, 2004.

"Let's Do the Numbers Rumba." *Rise and Shine*. Raffi. Cambridge, Mass.: Rounder Records, 1996.

"Let's Make Some Noise." *Everything Grows*. Raffi. Cambridge, Mass.: Rounder Records, 1987.

"Little Bird, Little Bird." *You Are My Little Bird*. Elizabeth Mitchell. Washington, D.C.: Smithsonian Folkways Recordings, 2006.

"The Little Turtle." *A Twinkle in Your Eye*. Burl Ives. New York: Sony Wonder, 1997.

"The Little White Duck." *Everything Grows*. Raffi. Cambridge, Mass.: Rounder Records, 1987.

"Little Wing." *You Are My Little Bird*. Elizabeth Mitchell. Washington, D.C.: Smithsonian Folkways Recordings, 2006.

"Magic Penny." *A Cathy and Marcy Collection for Kids*. Cathy Fink. Cambridge, Mass.: Rounder Records, 1994.

"Mary Wore Her Red Dress." *Quiet Time*. Raffi. Cambridge, Mass.: Rounder Records, 2006.

"Me and My Teddy Bear." *Teddy Bear Tunes*. Georgiana Liccione Stewart. Long Branch, N.J.: Kimbo Educational, 2003

"Milkshake Song." *Songs for Wiggleworms*. Chicago: Old Town School of Folk Music, 2000.

"Monkey See, Monkey Do." *Makin' Music: Boogie to the Beat*. Media, Pa.: Makin' Music Rockin' Rhythms, 2003.

"The More We Get Together." *Singable Songs Collection*. Raffi. Cambridge, Mass.: Rounder Records, 1996.

"Mr. Sun." *Singable Songs Collection*. Raffi. Cambridge, Mass.: Rounder Records, 1996.

"My Bonnie Lies over the Ocean." *Cheerful Baby*. Alpharetta, Ga.: Brainy Baby, 2006.

"My Dog Rags." *Kids Songs 2*. Nancy Cassidy. Palo Alto, Calif.: Klutz, 1986.

"Nursery Rhyme Instrumental." *Rise and Shine*. Raffi. Cambridge, Mass.: Rounder Records, 1996.

"Nursery Rhyme Medley." *Quiet Time*. Raffi. Cambridge, Mass.: Rounder Records, 2006.

"Octopus's Garden." *All You Need Is Love*. Redway, Calif.: Music for Little People, Distributed by Kid Rhino, 1999.

"Old MacDonald Had a Farm." *101 Toddler Favorites*. Redway, Calif.: Music for Little People, 2003.

"Peanut Butter and Jelly." *Songs for Wiggleworms*. Chicago: Old Town School of Folk Music, 2000.

"Peek-a-Boo." *Baby-O!* MaryLee Sunseri. Pacific Grove, Calif.: Piper Grove Music, 2005.

"Pop Goes the Weasel." *Toddler Tunes: 25 Classic Songs for Toddlers*. Franklin, Tenn.: Cedarmont Kids, 2004.

"Pumpkin, Pumpkin." *Wee Sing for Halloween*. Pamela Beall. New York: Price Stern Sloan, 2000.

"Pussy Cat, Pussy Cat." *Mainly Mother Goose*. Sharon, Lois, and Bram. Toronto: Elephant Records; Los Angeles: Drive Entertainment, 1994.

"Riding in an Airplane." *One Light, One Sun*. Raffi. Cambridge, Mass.: Rounder Records, 1985.

"Rock and Roll Freeze Dance." *So Big: Activity Songs for Little Ones*. Hap Palmer. Topanga, Calif.: Hap-Pal Music, 1994.

"Roll Over." *Toddler Tunes: 25 Classic Songs for Toddlers*. Franklin, Tenn.: Cedarmont Kids, 2004.

"Shake It Up." *Hunk-Ta-Bunk-Ta Funsies 2*. Katherine Dines. Denver: Hunk-Ta-Bunk-Ta Music, 2004.

"Shake My Sillies Out." *More Singable Songs*. Raffi. Universal City, Calif.: Shoreline/MCA Records, 1977.

"Sing a Song of Sixpence." *101 Toddler Favorites*. Redway, Calif.: Music for Little People, 2003.

"Six Little Ducks." *Toddler Tunes: 25 Classic Songs for Toddlers*. Franklin, Tenn.: Cedarmont Kids, 2004.

"Skinnamarink." *Great Big Hits*. Sharon, Lois, and Bram. Toronto: Elephant Records/A&M, 1992.

"So Happy You're Here." *So Big: Activity Songs for Little Ones*. Hap Palmer. Topanga, Calif.: Hap-Pal Music, 1994.

"Storytime Is over Now." *Preschool Favorites: 35 Storytimes Kids Love*. Diane Briggs. Chicago: ALA Editions, 2007.

"Teddy Bear Hug." *Everything Grows*. Raffi. Cambridge, Mass.: Rounder Records, 1987.

"Teddy Bear Playtime." *So Big: Activity Songs for Little Ones*. Hap Palmer. Topanga, Calif.: Hap-Pal Music, 1994.

"Teddy Bears' Picnic." *Teddy Bear Tunes*. Georgiana Liccione Stewart. Long Branch, N.J.: Kimbo Educational, 2003.

"This Little Light of Mine." *101 Toddler Favorites*. Redway, Calif.: Music for Little People, 2003.

"This Old Man." *Toddler Tunes: 25 Classic Songs for Toddlers*. Franklin, Tenn.: Cedarmont Kids, 2004.

"Three Blind Mice." *Mainly Mother Goose*. Sharon, Lois, and Bram. Toronto: Elephant Records; Los Angeles: Drive Entertainment, 1994.

"Three Little Birds." *You Are My Little Bird*. Elizabeth Mitchell. Washington, D.C.: Smithsonian Folkways Recordings, 2006.

"Three Little Fishies." *Three Silly Little Kittens*. Long Branch, N.J.: Kimbo Educational, 2002.

"Three Little Kittens." *Mainly Mother Goose*. Sharon, Lois, and Bram. Toronto: Elephant Records; Los Angeles: Drive Entertainment, 1994.

"Tiny Tim the Turtle." *Dr. Jean Sings Silly Songs*. Jean Feldman. Tampa, Fla.: Progressive Music Studios, 1999.

"Under the Sea." *The Little Mermaid*. Burbank, Calif.: Walt Disney Records, 1989.

"What'll I Do with the Baby-O?" *Baby-O!* MaryLee Sunseri. Pacific Grove, Calif.: Piper Grove Music, 2005.

"Wheels on the Bus." *Raffi's Box of Sunshine*. Raffi. Cambridge, Mass.: Rounder Records, 2000.

"Where Oh Where Has My Little Dog Gone?" *Toddler Tunes: 25 Classic Songs for Toddlers*. Franklin, Tenn.: Cedarmont Kids, 2004.

"Who Stole the Cookies?" *Silly Favorites*. Redway, Calif.: Music for Little People, Distributed by Kid Rhino, 1998.

"You Are My Sunshine." *Go Baby Go!* Baby Loves Jazz (Musical Group). New York: Verve Music, 2006.

Bibliography

Adams, Pam. *This Old Man*. Auburn, Me.: Child's Play, 2001.

Alborough, Jez. *Hug*. Cambridge, Mass.: Candlewick, 2000.

Alborough, Jez. *Tall*. Cambridge, Mass.: Candlewick, 2005.

Anholt, Catherine. *Bear and Baby*. Cambridge, Mass.: Candlewick, 1993.

Applet, Kathi. *Rain Dance*. New York: HarperFestival, 2001.

Ashman, Linda. *Babies on the Go*. San Diego, Calif.: Harcourt, 2003.

Baker, Keith. *Big Fat Hen*. San Diego, Calif.: Harcourt Brace, 1994.

Baker, Keith. *Hickory Dickory Dock*. Orlando, Fla.: Harcourt, 2007.

Barner, Bob. *Fish Wish*. New York: Holiday House, 2000.

Barry, Frances. *Duckie's Rainbow*. Cambridge, Mass.: Candlewick, 2004.

Barry, Frances. *Duckie's Splash*. Cambridge, Mass.: Candlewick, 2006.

Barton, Byron. *My Car*. New York: Greenwillow, 2001.

Bauer, Marion Dane. *My Mother Is Mine*. New York: Simon and Schuster, 2001.

Bauer, Marion Dane. *The Very Best Daddy of All*. New York: Simon and Schuster, 2004.

Beaumont, Karen. *Baby Danced the Polka*. New York: Dial, 2004.

Blackstone, Stella. *Bear at Home*. New York: Barefoot, 2001.

Bogacki, Tomek. *Cat and Mouse in the Snow*. New York: Farrar, Straus and Giroux, 1999.

Bogacki, Tomek. *Cat and Mouse*. New York: Farrar, Straus and Giroux. 1996.

Bornstein, Ruth. *Little Gorilla*. New York: Houghton Mifflin, 2000.

Braun, Sebastien. *I Love My Daddy*. New York: HarperCollins, 2004.

Braun, Sebastien. *I Love My Mommy*. New York: HarperCollins, 2004.

Brown, Margaret Wise. *The Golden Egg Book*. New York: Golden, 1947.

Brown, Margaret Wise. *The Runaway Bunny*. New York: HarperCollins, 1942.

Bryant, Lorinda Cauley. *Clap Your Hands*. New York: Putnam, 1992.

Butler, John. *Can You Cuddle Like a Koala?* Atlanta: Peachtree, 2003.

Butler, John. *Ten in the Den*. Atlanta: Peachtree, 2005.

Butler, John. *Ten in the Meadow*. Atlanta: Peachtree, 2006.

Butler, John. *Who Says Woof?* New York: Viking, 2003.

Butler, John. *Whose Baby Am I?* New York: Viking, 2001.

Cabrera, Jane. *Rory and the Lion*. New York: DK Publishing, 1999.

Cabrera, Jane. *Cat's Colors*. New York: Dial, 1997.

Cabrera, Jane. *Dog's Day*. New York: Orchard, 2000.

Campbell, Rod. *Dear Zoo*. New York: Four Winds, 1983.

Carle, Eric. *From Head to Toe*. New York: HarperCollins, 1997.

Carle, Eric. *Mr. Seahorse*. New York: Philomel, 2004.

Carle, Eric. *Papa, Please Get the Moon for Me*. New York: Simon and Schuster, 1986.

Carle, Eric. *The Very Hungry Caterpillar*. New York: Philomel, 1969.

Carlstrom, Nancy White. *Jesse Bear, What Will You Wear?* New York: Collier Macmillan, 1986.

Carroll, Kathleen Sullivan. *One Red Rooster*. Boston: Houghton Mifflin, 1992.

Carter, David. *If You're Happy and You Know It: A Pop-up Book*. New York: Scholastic, 1997.

Casey, Patricia. *My Cat Jack*. London: Walker, 2004.

Cauley, Lorinda Bryan. *Clap Your Hands*. New York: Putnam, 1992.

Christelow, Eilene. *Five Little Monkeys Jumping on the Bed*. New York: Clarion, 1989.

Christelow, Eilene. *Five Little Monkeys Sitting in a Tree*. New York: Clarion, 1991.

Cimarusti, Marie Torres. *Peek-a-Moo*. New York: Dutton Children's Books, 1998.

Cousins, Lucy. *Hooray for Fish!* Cambridge, Mass.: Candlewick, 2005.

Cousins, Lucy. *Maisy's Rainbow Dream*. Cambridge, Mass.: Candlewick, 2003.

Cousins, Lucy. *Maisy's Wonderful Weather Book*. Cambridge, Mass.: Candlewick, 2006.

Cowell, Cressida. *What Shall We Do with the Boo Hoo Baby?* New York: Scholastic, 2000.

Crews, Donald. *Freight Train*. New York: Greenwillow, 1978.

Cronin, Doreen. *Wiggle*. New York: Atheneum, 2005.

Dann, Penny. *Teddy Bear, Teddy Bear, Turn Around*. Hauppauge, N.Y.: Barron's Educational Series, 2001.

Degen, Bruce. *Jamberry*. New York: Harper and Row, 1983.

Demarest, Chris. *Honk!* Honesdale, Pa.: Boyds Mills, 1998.

Denchfield, Nick. *Charlie Chick: A Pop-up Book*. New York: Red Wagon, 2007.

Diamant-Cohen, Betsy. *Mother Goose on the Loose*. New York: Neal-Schuman, 2006.

Dodd, Emma. *Dog's Colorful Day*. New York: Dutton Children's Books, 2001.

Dodd, Emma. *Dog's Noisy Day*. New York: Dutton, 2003.

Dodd, Emma. *Yellow, Blue, and Bunny, Too! A Changing Picture Book of Colors*. New York: Dutton, 2001.

Dunrea, Olivier. *BooBoo*. Boston: Houghton Mifflin, 2004.

Durango, Julia. *Cha-cha Chimps*. New York: Simon and Schuster, 2006.

Ehlert, Lois. *Color Zoo*. New York: Lippincott, 1989.

Ehlert, Lois. *Feathers for Lunch*. San Diego, Calif.: Harcourt Brace Jovanovich, 1990.

Falwell, Cathryn. *Feast for 10*. New York: Houghton Mifflin, 1996.

Falwell, Cathryn. *Turtle Splash! Countdown at the Pond*. New York: Greenwillow, 2001.

Faulkner, Keith. *The Long-Nosed Pig*. New York: Dial Books for Young Readers, 1998.

Faulkner, Keith. *The Wide-Mouthed Frog: A Pop-up Book*. New York: Dial, 1996.

Feiffer, Jules. *Bark, George*. New York: HarperCollins, 1999.

Flack, Marjorie. *Ask Mr. Bear*. New York: Macmillan, 1932.

Fleming, Candace. *This Is the Baby*. New York: Melanie Kroupa, 2004.

Fleming, Denise. *Barnyard Banter*. New York: Holt, 1994.

Fleming, Denise. *Lunch*. New York: Holt, 1993.

Florian, Douglas. *Turtle Day*. New York: Crowell, 1989.

Ford, Bernette G. *No More Diapers for Ducky*. London: Boxer, 2006.

Fox, Mem. *Boo to a Goose*. New York: Dial, 1998.

Fox, Mem. *Where Is the Green Sheep?* Orlando, Fla.: Harcourt, 2004.

Gag, Wanda. *ABC Bunny*. New York: Coward, McCann and Geoghegan, 1933.

Genechten, Guido van. *Because I Love You So Much*. Wilton, Conn.: Tiger Tales, 2004.

Ginsburg, Mirra. *Good Morning, Chick*. New York: Greenwillow, 1980.

Greenfield, Eloise. *Water, Water*. New York: HarperFestival, 1999.

Gutman, Anne. *Daddy Cuddles*. San Francisco: Chronicle, 2005.

Gutman, Anne. *Daddy Kisses*. San Francisco: Chronicle, 2003.

Gutman, Anne. *Mommy Hugs*. San Francisco: Chronicle, 2003.

Gutman, Anne. *Mommy Loves*. San Francisco: Chronicle, 2005.

Hale, Sarah Josepha Buell. *Mary Had a Little Lamb*. New York: Orchard, 1995.

Hall, Zoë. *It's Pumpkin Time*. New York: Scholastic, 1994.

Halpern, Shari. *Little Robin Redbreast*. New York: North-South, 1994.

Harper, Isabelle. *My Dog Rosie*. New York: Blue Sky, 1994.

Heap, Sue. *Bug in a Rug: A Lift-the-Flap Colors Book*. New York: Puffin, 2000.

Hey, Diddle, Diddle: A Children's Book of Nursery Rhymes. New York: Holt, 2003.

Hill, Eric. *Spot Bakes a Cake*. New York: Putnam, 1994.

Hill, Eric. *Spot's Halloween*. New York: Putnam, 2003.

Hill, Eric. *Where's Spot?* New York: Putnam, 1980.

Hindley, Judy. *Do Like Duck Does*. Cambridge, Mass.: Candlewick, 2002.

Holub, Joan. *Eek-a-Boo! A Spooky Lift-a-Flap Book*. New York: Scholastic, 2000.

Hort, Lenny. *Seals on the Bus*. New York: Holt, 2000.

Hort, Lenny. *We're Going on a Safari*. New York: Harry N. Abrams, 2002.

Hutchins, Pat. *Rosie's Walk*. New York: Macmillan, 1968.

Intrater, Roberta Grobel. *Peek-a-Boo, You!* New York: Scholastic, 2002.

Isadora, Rachel. *I Hear*. New York: Greenwillow, 1985.

Kalan, Robert. *Blue Sea*. New York: Scholastic, 1979.

Kalan, Robert. *Rain*. New York: Greenwillow, 1978.

Kalan, Robert. *Jump, Frog, Jump!* New York: Greenwillow, 1981.

Karas, Brian G. *Skidamarink: A Silly Love Song to Sing Together*. New York: HarperFestival, 2002.

Katz, Karen. *Counting Kisses*. New York: McElderry, 2001.

Katz, Karen. *Daddy and Me: A Lift-a-Flap Book*. New York: Little Simon, 2003.

Katz, Karen. *Daddy Hugs 1, 2, 3*. New York: McElderry, 2005.

Katz, Karen. *Daddy Hugs*. New York: Little Simon, 2007.

Katz, Karen. *Mommy Hugs*. New York: McElderry, 2006.

Katz, Karen. *Peek-a-Baby: A Lift-a-Flap Book*. New York: Little Simon, 2007.

Katz, Karen. *What Does Baby Say?* New York: Little Simon, 2004.

Katz, Karen. *Where Is Baby's Belly Button?* New York: Little Simon, 2000.

Katz, Karen. *Where Is Baby's Mommy?* New York: Little Simon 2000.

Katz, Karen. *Where Is Baby's Pumpkin? A Lift-the-Flap Book*. New York: Little Simon, 2006.

Katz, Karen. *Where Is Baby's Valentine?* New York: Little Simon, 2006.

Kelly, Martin. *Five Green and Speckled Frogs*. New York: Handprint, 2000.

Kopper, Lisa. *Daisy's Babies*. New York: Dutton, 2000.

Kuskin, Karla. *Roar and More*. New York: Harper and Row, 1990.

Kutner, Merrily. *Down on the Farm*. New York: Holiday House, 2004.

Lawrence, John. *This Little Chick*. Cambridge, Mass.: Candlewick, 2002.

Lawrence, Michael. *Baby Loves*. New York: DK Publishing, 1999.

Lee, Kate. *Snappy Little Colors*. San Diego, Calif.: Silver Dolphin, 2002.

Lee, Kate. *Snappy Little Numbers*. Brookfield, Conn.: Millbrook, 1998.

Leslie, Amanda. *Flappy, Waggy, Wiggly*. New York: Dutton, 1999.

Lewis, Kevin. *Tugga Tugga Tugboat*. New York: Hyperion, 2006.

Lewis, Kevin. *Chugga-Chugga Choo-Choo*. New York: Hyperion, 1999.

Linch, Tanya. *Three Little Kittens*. Columbus, Ohio: Gingham Dog, 2007.

MacDonald, Suse. *Sea Shapes*. San Diego, Calif.: Harcourt Brace, 1994.

MacKinnon, Debbie. *Meg's Monkey: A Lift-a-Flap Board Book*. New York: Dial, 1996.

Martin, Bill. *Brown Bear, Brown Bear, What Do You See?* New York: Holt, 1992.

Martin, Bill. *Here Are My Hands*. New York: Holt, 1985.

Martin, Bill. *Polar Bear, Polar Bear, What Do You Hear?* New York: Holt, 1991.

Martin, David. *We've All Got Bellybuttons!* Cambridge, Mass.: Candlewick, 2005.

Matthew, Derek. *Snappy Sounds Roar!* Berkeley, Calif.: Silver Dolphin, 2004.

McDonnell, Flora. *Splash!* Cambridge, Mass.: Candlewick, 1999.

McGee, Marni. *The Noisy Farm*. New York: Bloomsbury Children's Books, 2004.

Miller, Virginia. *I Love You Just the Way You Are*. Cambridge, Mass.: Candlewick, 1998.

Miller, Virginia. *Ten Red Apples*. Cambridge, Mass.: Candlewick, 2002.

Minarik, Else Holmelund. *A Kiss for Little Bear*. New York: HarperTrophy, 1984.

Most, Bernard. *Cock-a-Doodle-Moo!* San Diego, Calif.: Harcourt Brace, 1996.

My Very First Mother Goose. Cambridge, Mass.: Candlewick, 1996.

Numeroff, Laura. *If You Give a Mouse a Cookie*. New York: Harper and Row, 1985.

O'Connell, Rebecca. *The Baby Goes Beep*. Brookfield, Conn.: Roaring Brook, 2003.

O'Keefe, Susan Heyboer. *Love Me, Love You*. Honesdale, Pa.: Boyds Mills, 2001.

Oxenbury, Helen. *Tom and Pippo on the Beach*. Cambridge, Mass.: Candlewick, 1993.

Parker, Victoria. *Bearobics: A Hip-Hop Counting Story*. New York: Viking, 1997.

Parr, Todd. *The Mommy Book*. Boston: Little, Brown, 2002.

Peek, Merle. *Roll Over: A Counting Song*. New York: Houghton Mifflin/Clarion, 1981.

Pilkey, Dav. *The Complete Adventures of Big Dog and Little Dog*. New York: Harcourt, 2003.

Polushkin, Maria. *Mother, Mother, I Want Another*. New York: Knopf, 2005.

Porter-Gaylord, Laurel. *I Love My Daddy Because*. New York: Dutton, 1991.

Porter-Gaylord, Laurel. *I Love My Mommy Because*. New York: Dutton, 1991.

Rathmann, Peggy. *Good Night, Gorilla*. New York: Putnam, 1994.

Ray, Mary Lyn. *Red Rubber Boot Day*. Orlando, Fla.: Harcourt, 2005.

Rice, Eve. *Sam Who Never Forgets*. New York: Morrow, 1977.

Riley, Linnea. *Mouse Mess*. New York: Blue Sky, 1997.

Robart, Rose. *The Cake That Mack Ate*. Boston: Little, Brown, 1986.

Roddie, Shen. *Hatch, Egg, Hatch!* Boston: Little, Brown, 1990.

Saltzberg, Barney. *I Love Dogs*. Cambridge, Mass.: Candlewick, 2005.

Schindel, John. *Busy Monkeys*. Berkeley, Calif.: Tricycle, 2002.

Scott, Michael. *Five Little Pumpkins*. New York: Hyperion, 2003.

Scott, Steve. *Teddy Bear, Teddy Bear*. New York: HarperFestival, 1998.

Shannon, David. *Oops!* New York: Blue Sky, 2005.

Simmons, Jane. *Daisy's Hide-and-Seek: A Lift-the-Flap Book*. Boston: Little, Brown, 2001.

Sis, Peter. *Fire Truck*. New York: Greenwillow, 1998.

Smee, Nicola. *Clip-Clop*. New York: Boxer, 2006.

Spence, Robert. *Clickety Clack*. New York: Viking, 1999.

Steer, Dugald. *Snappy Little Farmyard: Spend a Day Down on Noisy Farm*. Brookfield, Conn.: Millbrook, 1999.

Stenmark, Victoria. *The Singing Chick*. New York: Holt, 1999.

Stickland, Paul. *One Bear, One Dog*. New York: Dutton, 1997.

Stickland, Paul. *Ten Terrible Dinosaurs*. New York: Dutton, 1997.

Stickland, Paul. *Truck Jam!* New York: Ragged Bears, 2000.

Stott, Dorothy. *Bingo (Sing-a-Story)*. Columbus, Ohio: School Specialty, 2006.

Sturges, Philemon. *I Love Trains*. New York: HarperFestival, 2006.

Tafuri, Nancy. *Early Morning in the Barn*. New York: Greenwillow, 1983.

Tafuri, Nancy. *Goodnight, My Duckling*. New York: Scholastic, 2005.

Tafuri, Nancy. *Silly Little Goose!* New York: Scholastic, 2001.

Tafuri, Nancy. *Spots, Feathers, and Curly Tails*. New York: Greenwillow, 1988.

Tafuri, Nancy. *What the Sun Sees*. New York: Greenwillow, 1997.

Tafuri, Nancy. *Whose Chick Are You?* New York: Greenwillow, 2007.

Taylor, Jane. *Twinkle, Twinkle, Little Star*. San Francisco: Chronicle, 2001.

Thompson, Kim Mitzo. *Five Little Monkeys Jumping on the Bed (Sing-a-Story)*. Columbus, Ohio: School Specialty, 2006.

Thompson, Kim Mitzo. *Six Little Ducks (Sing-a-Story)*. Columbus, Ohio: School Specialty, 2006.

Thompson, Lauren. *Little Quack*. New York: Little Simon, 2005.

Thompson, Lauren. *Little Quack's New Friend*. New York: Simon and Schuster, 2006.

Thompson, Lauren. *Mouse's First Valentine*. New York: Simon and Schuster, 2002.

Timmers, Leo. *Who Is Driving?* New York: Bloomsbury, 2007.

Titherington, Jean. *Pumpkin, Pumpkin*. New York: Greenwillow, 1986.

Van Laan, Nancy. *Scrubba Dub*. New York: Atheneum, 2003.

Van Laan, Nancy. *Little Fish Lost*. New York: Atheneum, 1998.

Van Laan, Nancy. *The Big Fat Worm*. New York: Knopf, 1987.

Van Laan, Nancy. *Tickle Tum!* New York: Atheneum, 2001.

Van Rynbach, Iris. *Five Little Pumpkins*. Honesdale, Pa.: Boyds Mills, 1995.

Waddell, Martin. *Hi, Harry!* Cambridge, Mass.: Candlewick, 2003.

Waddell, Martin. *Owl Babies*. Cambridge, Mass.: Candlewick, 1992.

Walsh, Ellen Stoll. *Mouse Paint*. New York: Red Wagon, 1991.

Walsh, Melanie. *Do Monkeys Tweet?* Boston: Houghton Mifflin, 1997.

Watanabe, Shigeo. *Daddy, Play with Me*. New York: Philomel, 1985.

Watanabe, Shigeo. *How Do I Put It On?* New York: Philomel, 1992.

Watanabe, Shigeo. *What a Good Lunch!* New York: Philomel, 1980.

Watanabe, Shigeo. *Where's My Daddy?* New York: Philomel, 1982.

Watt, Fiona. *Cuddly Baby*. Tulsa, Okla.: Usborne, 2006.

Watt, Fiona. *That's Not My Bunny*. Tulsa, Okla.: Usborne, 2005.

Watt, Fiona. *That's Not My Puppy*. Tulsa, Okla.: Usborne, 2001.

Watt, Fiona. *That's Not My Teddy*. Tulsa, Okla.: Usborne, 2000.

Watt, Fiona. *That's Not My Kitten*. Tulsa, Okla.: EDC Publishers, 2001.

Weatherford, Carole Boston. *Jazz Baby*. New York: Lee and Low, 2002.

Weeks, Sarah. *Overboard!* Orlando, Fla.: Harcourt, 2006.

Weeks, Sarah. *Ruff! Ruff! Where's Scruff?* San Diego, Calif.: Red Wagon, 2006.

Wellington, Monica. *All My Little Ducklings*. New York: Dutton, 1995.

Wells, Rosemary. *Read to Your Bunny*. New York: Scholastic, 1997.

Whybrow, Ian. *The Noisy Way to Bed*. New York: Arthur A. Levine, 2004.

Willems, Mo. *Knuffle Bunny: A Cautionary Tale*. New York: Hyperion, 2004.

Williams, Sue. *I Went Walking*. San Diego, Calif.: Harcourt Brace and Company, 1990.

Wilson, Karma. *Bear Snores On*. New York: McElderry, 2002.

Wilson, Karma. *Bear Wants More*. New York: McElderry, 2003.

Wilson, Karma. *Bear's New Friend*. New York: McElderry, 2006.

Wilson, Karma. *Hello, Calico!* New York: Little Simon, 2007.

Wojtowycz, David. *Can You Choo Choo?* New York: Scholastic, 2003.

Wojtowycz, David. *Can You Moo?* New York: Scholastic, 2003.

Wood, Audrey. *Quick as a Cricket*. Singapore: Child's Play, 1982.

Wood, Audrey. *Silly Sally*. San Diego, Calif.: Harcourt Brace Jovanovich, 1991.

Wood, Audrey. *Ten Little Fish*. New York: Blue Sky, 2004.

Wood, Don. *The Little Mouse, the Red Ripe Strawberry, and the Big Hungry Bear*. New York: Scholastic, 1994.

Wu, Norbert. *Fish Faces*. New York: Holt, 1993.

Yaccarino, Dan. *An Octopus Followed Me Home*. New York: Viking, 1997.

Yolen, Jane. *Dimity Duck*. New York: Philomel, 2006.

Yolen, Jane. *Mouse's Birthday*. New York: Putnam, 1993.

Index

ABC Bunny (book), 1
Adams, Pam, 49, 83
"A-Goong Went the Little Green Frog" (song), 124
Airplanes (rhyme), 130
Alborough, Jez, 35, 59
All for Baby (rhyme), 134
All My Little Ducklings (book), 23
"All You Need Is Love" (song), 36
Anholt, Catherine, 117
Applet, Kathi, 91
Ashman, Linda, 133
Ask Mr. Bear (book), 36
Ask Mr. Bear (flannel-board story), 36
"At the Zoo" (song), 28

"Baa, Baa, Black Sheep" (song), 8
Babies on the Go (book), 133
"Baby Beluga" (song), 18
"Baby Chickie" (song), 2
Baby Danced the Polka (book), 133
The Baby Goes Beep (book), 75, 133
Baby Loves (book), 35, 133
Baby's Nap (rhyme), 133
Baker, Keith, 13, 83, 111
Bark, George (book), 101
Barner, Bob, 17
Barnyard Banter (book), 7
Barry, Frances, 13, 23, 91, 95
Barton, Byron, 129
Bauer, Marion Dane, 65, 71
Bear and Baby (book), 117

Bear at Home (book), 117
Bear in a Cave (rhyme), 118
Bear Snores On (book), 117
Bear Wants More (book), 117
"The Bear Went over the Mountain" (song), 118
Bearobics: A Hip-Hop Counting Story (book), 49, 117
Bear's New Friend (book), 117
Beaumont, Karen, 133
Because I Love You So Much (book), 35, 117
Big Fat Hen (book), 13
The Big Fat Worm (book), 14
The Big Fat Worm (flannel-board story), 14
Bingo (Sing-a-Story) (book), 101
Blackstone, Stella, 117
Blue Sea (book), 17
"Bluebird" (song), 14
Bogacki, Tomek, 111
Boo to a Goose (book), 13
BooBoo (book), 143
Bornstein, Ruth, 59
bouncing bug (craft), 110
Bouncy Ball (rhyme), 49
The Boy in the Barn (rhyme), 8
Braun, Sebastien, 65, 71
Brown Bear, Brown Bear, What Do You See? (book), 95
Brown, Margaret Wise, 1, 71
Bryant, Lorinda Cauley, 75
Bug in a Rug: A Lift-the-Flap Colors Book (book), 95
"Bumping Up and Down" (song), 130
Bumpity Pumpkin (rhyme), 41

Busy Monkeys (book), 59
Butler, John, 49, 55, 75, 133

Cabrera, Jane, 27, 95, 101, 111
The Cake That Mack Ate (book), 102, 143
The Cake That Mack Ate (flannel-board story), 102
Campbell, Rod, 27
Can You Choo Choo? (book), 75, 129
Can You Cuddle Like a Koala? (book), 55
Can You Moo? (book), 7, 75
cardboard tube kazoo (craft), 76
Carle, Eric, 17, 27, 55, 65, 143
Carlstrom, Nancy White, 117
Carringer, Josephine Judson, 18
Carroll, Kathleen Sullivan, 7, 49
Carter, David, 55
"Carving Pumpkins" (song), 42
Casey, Patricia, 111
Cat and Mouse (book), 111
Cat and Mouse in the Snow (book), 111
Catching a Fish (rhyme), 18, 49
Cat's Colors (book), 95, 111
Cauley, Lorinda Bryan, 55
Cha-Cha Chimps (book), 109
Charlie Chick: A Pop-Up Book (book), 1, 7
Choo-Choo Train (rhyme), 75, 130
Christelow, Eileen, 59, 109
Chugga-Chugga Choo-Choo (book), 129
Cimarusti, Marie Torres, 7, 27, 75, 109
circus train (craft), 130
Clap Your Hands (book), 55, 75
Clickety Clack (book), 129
Clip-Clop (book), 7
Cock-a-Doodle-Moo! (book), 7
Color Zoo (book), 27
Colors (rhyme), 95
"Colors" (song), 96
The Complete Adventures of Big Dog and Little Dog (book), 101
cookies (craft), 144
counting caterpillar (craft), 50
Counting Kisses (book), 35, 49, 71
Cousins, Lucy, 17, 91, 95
Cowell, Cressida, 133
Crews, Donald, 130
Criss, Cross, Applesauce (rhyme), 109
Cronin, Doreen, 109
Cuddly Baby (book), 133
cut-out flowers (craft), 135

Daddy and Me: A Lift-a-Flap Book (book), 65
Daddy Cuddles (book), 65
Daddy Hugs (book), 35
Daddy Hugs 1, 2, 3 (book), 65
Daddy Kisses (book), 65
Daddy, Play with Me (book), 65
"Daddy-o" (song), 66
daisies for Mom (craft), 72
Daisy's Babies (book), 101
Daisy's Hide-and-Seek: A Lift-the-Flap Book (book), 23
Dalmatian puppy (craft), 96
Dann, Penny, 117
Dear Zoo (book), 27
Degen, Bruce, 143
Demarest, Chris, 13
Denchfield, Nick, 1, 7
Diamant-Cohen, Betsy, 83
Digging in the Dirt (rhyme), 101
Dimity Duck (book), 23, 123
Do Like Duck Does (book), 23
Do Monkeys Tweet? (book), 27, 75
"Do Your Ears Hang Low?" (song), 102
Dodd, Emma, 75, 95, 101
Dog's Colorful Day (book), 96, 101
Dog's Colorful Day (flannel-board story), 96
Dog's Day (book), 101
Dog's Noisy Day (book), 75
"Down by the Station" (song), 130
"Down on Grandpa's Farm" (song), 8
Down on the Farm (book), 7
Duckie's Rainbow (book), 13, 23, 91, 95
Duckie's Splash (book), 23
"Ducks Like Rain" (song), 24
Dunrea, Olivier, 143
Durango, Julia, 109

Early Morning in the Barn (book), 7
Eek-a-Boo! A Spooky Lift-a-Flap Book (book), 41
Eensy, Weensy Spider (rhyme), 91
egg bunny (craft), 2
egg-carton mouse (craft), 112
Ehlert, Lois, 13, 27
The Elephant and the Bad Baby (flannel-board story), 134
Elephant Walks (rhyme), 27

Falwell, Cathryn, 123, 143
Faulkner, Keith, 7, 123

Feast for 10 (book), 143
feathered friend (craft), 14
Feathers for Lunch (book), 13
Feiffer, Jules, 101
Finger Family (rhyme), 65
Fire Truck (book), 129
fish and pole (craft), 66
Fish Faces (book), 17
Fish Wish (book), 17
fish with shiny scales (craft), 19
Five Funny Dinosaurs (flannel-board song), 5
Five Green and Speckled Frogs (book), 123
"Five Green Speckled Frogs" (song), 124
Five Little Cookies (flannel-board rhyme), 144
"Five Little Ducks" (song), 24, 72
Five Little Ducks Went in for a Swim (rhyme), 23
Five Little Fishes (rhyme), 17
Five Little Green Frogs (rhyme), 124
Five Little Ice Creams (flannel-board rhyme), 144
Five Little Monkeys (rhyme), 28, 109
Five Little Monkeys and the Crocodile (rhyme), 59
Five Little Monkeys Jumping on the Bed (book), 59, 109
Five Little Monkeys Jumping on the Bed (flannel-board rhyme), 60, 110
Five Little Monkeys Jumping on the Bed (Sing-a-Story) (book), 59
Five Little Monkeys Sitting in a Tree (book), 59
Five Little Pumpkins (book), 41
Five Little Pumpkins (rhyme), 42
"Five Little Pumpkins" (song), 42
Five Little Pumpkins in a Pumpkin Patch (flannel-board rhyme), 42
Flack, Marjorie, 36
Flappy, Waggy, Wiggly (book), 27
Fleming, Candace, 133
Fleming, Denise, 7, 95, 111, 143
Florian, Douglas, 123
Ford, Bernette G., 23
Fox, Mem, 13, 95
Freight Train (book), 130
Freight Train (flannel-board story), 130
"Frog Went a-Courting" (song), 124
From Head to Toe (book), 27, 55
Funny Ducky (rhyme), 23
"Funny Little Bunny" (song), 2

Gag, Wanda, 1
Genechten, Guido van, 35, 117

Ginsburg, Mirra, 1
"Going to the Zoo" (song), 28
The Golden Egg Book (book), 1
Good Morning, Chick (book), 1
"Good Morning, Merry Sunshine" (song), 92
Good Night, Gorilla (book), 27, 59
"Goodbye Song" (song), xi
Goodnight, My Duckling (book), 23
Greenfield, Eloise, 91
Gutman, Anne, 65, 71

Had a Little Rooster (flannel-board song), 8
"Had a Little Rooster" (song), 76
Hale, Sarah Josepha Buell, 83
Hall, Zoë, 41
Halpern, Shari, 13
Harper, Isabelle, 101
Hatch, Egg, Hatch! (book), 1
"Head, Shoulders, Knees, and Toes" (song), 110
Heap, Sue, 95
heart puppet (craft), 36
Hello, Calico! (book), 111
Here Are My Hands (book), 55
Here Is a Bunny (rhyme), 1
Here Is a Little Girl (rhyme), 65
Here Is a Nest for a Robin (rhyme), 13
"Here Sits a Monkey" (song), 60
"Here's a Ball for Baby" (song), 134
Hey Diddle Diddle (flannel-board rhyme), 84
"Hey, Diddle, Diddle" (song), 8
Hey, Diddle, Diddle: A Children's Book of Nursery Rhymes (book), 83
Hi, Harry! (book), 123
Hickory Dickory Dock (book), 83, 111
"Hickory, Dickory, Dock" (song), 112
Hill, Eric, 41, 101, 143
Hindley, Judy, 23
Holub, Joan, 41
Honk! (book), 13
Hooray for Fish! (book), 17
Hop, Little Bunny (rhyme), 1
Hort, Lenny, 27, 129
Hot Cross Buns (rhyme), 143
How Do I Put It On? (book), 56, 110
How Do I Put It On? (flannel-board story), 56, 110
Hug (book), 35, 59
Humpty Dumpty (flannel-board rhyme), 84
"Hush Little Baby" (song), 134
Hutchins, Pat, 13

I Hear (book), 55
I Love Dogs (book), 101
I Love Mommy (rhyme), 71
I Love My Daddy (book), 65
I Love My Daddy Because (book), 65
I Love My Mommy (book), 71
I Love My Mommy Because (book), 71
I Love Trains (book), 129
I Love You Just the Way You Are (book), 35, 117
I Went Walking (book), 55
"If All of the Raindrops" (song), 144
If You Give a Mouse a Cookie (book), 143
If You're Happy and You Know It: A Pop-Up Book
    (book), 55
I'm a Little Pumpkin (rhyme), 41
I'm a Little Teapot (rhyme), 144
I'm a Little Truck (rhyme), 129
I'm a Tiger (rhyme), 76
Intrater, Roberta Grobel, 55
Isadora, Rachel, 55
It's Pumpkin Time (book), 41
"It's Raining, It's Pouring" (song), 92
Itsy Bitsy Monkey (rhyme), 59

Jack and Jill (rhyme), 83
Jamberry (book), 143
Jazz Baby (book), 75
Jesse Bear, What Will You Wear? (book), 117
Jump, Frog, Jump! (book), 123
Jump, Frog, Jump! (flannel-board story), 124

Kalan, Robert, 17, 91, 123
Karas, Brian G., 35
Katz, Karen, 35, 41, 49, 65, 71, 133
Kelly, Martin, 123
A Kiss for Little Bear (book), 118
A Kiss for Little Bear (flannel-board story), 110, 118
Kitty Diddy, Diddy Dum Diddy Do (song), 112
Knuffle Bunny: A Cautionary Tale (book), 1
Kopper, Lisa, 101
Kuskin, Karla, 76
Kutner, Merrily, 7

lamb with clothespin legs (craft), 84
Lawrence, John, 1
Lawrence, Michael, 35, 133
Lee, Kate, 49, 95
Leslie, Amanda, 27
Let Me Hear You (rhyme), 2
"Let's Do the Numbers Rumba" (song), 50

Let's Hear You Roar! (rhyme), 76
"Let's Make Some Noise" (song), 76
Lewis, Kevin, 129
Linch, Tanya, 83
lion mask (craft), 28
"Little Bird, Little Bird" (song), 14
Little Birds Fly (rhyme), 14
Little Fish Lost (book), 17
Little Frog (rhyme), 124
Little Gorilla (book), 59
Little Heart (rhyme), 35
Little Kittens (rhyme), 111
Little Miss Muffett (flannel-board rhyme), 84
*The Little Mouse, the Red Ripe Strawberry, and the Big
    Hungry Bear* (book), 111
Little Mousie (rhyme), 111
Little Puppy (rhyme), 101
Little Quack (book), 23
Little Quack's New Friend (book), 123
Little Robin Redbreast (book), 13
"The Little Turtle" (song), 124
"The Little White Duck" (flannel-board song), 24
"The Little White Duck" (song), 24
"Little Wing" (song), 14
The Long-Nosed Pig (book), 7
Love Me, Love You (book), 1, 35
Lunch (book), 95, 111, 143
Lunch (flannel-board story), 112

MacDonald, Suse, 17
MacKinnon, Debbie, 59
"Magic Penny" (song), 36
Maisy's Rainbow Dream (book), 95
Maisy's Wonderful Weather Book (book), 91
Martin, Bill, 27, 55, 75, 95
Martin, David, 55
Mary Had a Little Lamb (book), 83
"Mary Wore Her Red Dress" (song), 96
Matthew, Derek, 75
McDonnell, Flora, 109
McGee, Marni, 75
"Me and My Teddy Bear" (song), 118
Meg's Monkey: A Lift-a-Flap Board Book (book),
    59
"Milkshake Song" (song), 144
Miller, Virginia, 35, 49, 117
Minarik, Else Holmelund, 118
The Mommy Book (book), 71
Mommy Hugs (book), 35, 71
Mommy Loves (book), 71

Monkey See, Monkey Do (rhyme), 60
"Monkey See, Monkey Do" (song), 60
"The More We Get Together" (song), xi
Most, Bernard, 7
mother duck and ducklings (craft), 24
Mother Goose on the Loose (book), 83
Mother, Mother, I Want Another (book), 72
Mother, Mother, I Want Another (flannel-board story), 72
Mouse Mess (book), 111
Mouse Paint (book), 95
Mouse's Birthday (book), 111
Mouse's First Valentine (book), 35
Mr. Seahorse (book), 17
"Mr. Sun" (song), 92
My Car (book), 129
My Cat Jack (book), 111
"My Daddy Is Really Quite Special" (song), 66
"My Dog Rags" (song), 102
My Dog Rosie (book), 101
My Mommy (rhyme), 71
My Mother Is Mine (book), 71
My Very First Mother Goose (book), 83

No More Diapers for Ducky (book), 23
The Noisy Farm (book), 75
The Noisy Way to Bed (book), 75
Numeroff, Laura, 143
"Nursery Rhyme Instrumental" (song), 84
"Nursery Rhyme Medley" (song), 84

O'Connell, Rebecca, 75, 133
An Octopus Followed Me Home (book), 109
"Octopus's Garden" (song), 18
O'Keefe, Susan Heyboer, 1, 35
"Old MacDonald Had a Farm" (song), 8
On the Farm (rhyme), 7
One Bear, One Dog (book), 101, 117
One Little Baby (rhyme), 134
One Red Rooster (book), 7, 49
Oops! (book), 109
Open and Shut Them (rhyme), 55
Overboard! (book), 109
Owl Babies (book), 13
Oxenbury, Helen, 59

Papa, Please Get the Moon for Me (book), 65
paper-bag puppy (craft), 102
paper-bag teddy bear (craft), 118
paper-bowl turtle (craft), 124

paper-cup rooster (craft), 9
Parker, Victoria, 49, 117
Parr, Todd, 71
Pat-a-Cake (rhyme), 133, 143
"Peanut Butter and Jelly" (song), 144
Peek, Merle, 49
Peek-a-Baby: A Lift-a-Flap Book (book), 133
"Peek-a-Boo" (song), 134
peek-a-boo pumpkin stick puppet (craft), 42
Peek-a-Boo, You! (book), 55
Peek-a-Moo! (book), 7, 75, 109
Peek-a-Zoo! (book), 27
A Perfect White Egg (rhyme), 2
picture of little, adorable me (craft), 56
Pilkey, Dav, 101
Polar Bear, Polar Bear, What Do You Hear? (book), 27, 75
"Pop Goes the Weasel" (song), 60
Porter-Gaylord, Laurel, 65, 71
Pumpkin, Pumpkin (book), 41
"Pumpkin, Pumpkin" (song), 42
"Pussy Cat, Pussy Cat" (song), 112
Pussycat, Pussycat (rhyme), 112

Quick as a Cricket (book), 55

Rain (book), 91
Rain (flannel-board story), 92
Rain (rhyme), 91
Rain Dance (book), 91
Rain on the Green Grass (rhyme), 91
Rainbow Colors (rhyme), 95
Rathmann, Peggy, 27, 59
Ray, Mary Lyn, 91
Read to Your Bunny (book), 1
Red Fish, Red Fish (flannel-board poem), 19
Red Rubber Boot Day (book), 91
Rice, Eve, 27
"Riding in an Airplane" (song), 130
Riley, Linnea, 111
Roar and More (book), 76
Roar and More (flannel-board story), 76
Robart, Rose, 102, 143
Roddie, Shen, 1
"Roll Over" (song), 50
Roll Over: A Counting Song (book), 49
Rory and the Lion (book), 27
Rosie's Walk (book), 13
Ruff! Ruff! Where's Scruff? (book), 101
The Runaway Bunny (book), 71

Saltzberg, Barney, 101
Sam Who Never Forgets (book), 27
Sam Who Never Forgets (flannel-board story), 28
Schindel, John, 59
Scott, Michael, 41
Scott, Steve, 117
Scrubba Dub (book), 1
Sea Shapes (book), 17
Seals on the Bus (book), 129
"Shake It Up" (song), xi
"Shake My Sillies Out" (song), xi, 110
Shannon, David, 109
Silly Little Goose! (book), 13, 109
Silly Sally (book), 109
Simmons, Jane, 23
"Sing a Song of Sixpence" (song), 14
The Singing Chick (book), 2
The Singing Chick (flannel-board story), 2
Sis, Peter, 129
Six Little Ducks (Sing-a-Story) (book), 23
"Six Little Ducks" (song), 24, 50
Skidamarink: A Silly Love Song to Sing Together (book), 35
"Skinnamarink" (song), 36
Slippery Fish (rhyme), 18
Smee, Nicola, 7
Snappy Little Colors (book), 95
Snappy Little Farmyard: Spend a Day Down on Noisy Farm (book), 7
Snappy Little Numbers (book), 49
Snappy Sounds Roar! (book), 75
"So Happy You're Here" (song), xi
Spence, Robert, 129
Splash! (book), 109
Spot Bakes a Cake (book), 143
Spots, Feathers, and Curly Tails (book), 7, 27
Spot's Halloween (book), 41
Spotted Giraffe (rhyme), 27
Steer, Dugald, 7
Stenmark, Victoria, 2
Stickland, Paul, 49, 101, 117, 129
"Storytime Is over Now" (song), xi
Stott, Dorothy, 101
Sturges, Philemon, 129
sun mask (craft), 92
"Sweet, Dear Mommy" (song), 72

Tafuri, Nancy, 7, 13, 23, 27, 91, 109
Tall (book), 59
Taylor, Jane, 83

Teddy Bear Dance (rhyme), 118
"Teddy Bear Hug" (song), 118
"Teddy Bear Playtime" (song), 118
Teddy Bear, Teddy Bear (book), 117
Teddy Bear, Teddy Bear (rhyme), 117
Teddy Bear, Teddy Bear, Turn Around (book), 117
"Teddy Bears' Picnic" (song), 118
"Teddy Wore His Red Shirt" (song), 96, 118
"Ten in the Bed" (song), 50
Ten in the Den (book), 49
Ten in the Meadow (book), 49
Ten Little Fish (book), 17
Ten Red Apples (book), 49
Ten Terrible Dinosaurs (book), 49
That's Not My Bunny (book), 1
That's Not My Kitten (book), 111
That's Not My Puppy (book), 101
That's Not My Teddy (book), 117
There Was a Little Turtle (rhyme), 123
This Is the Baby (book), 133
This Little Chick (book), 1
"This Little Light of Mine" (song), 56
This Old Man (book), 49, 83
"This Old Man" (song), 50
Thompson, Kim Mitzo, 23, 59
Thompson, Lauren, 23, 35, 123
"Three Blind Mice" (song), 112
"Three Little Birds" (song), 14
"Three Little Fishies" (song), 18
Three Little Kittens (book), 83
"Three Little Kittens" (song), 112
Tickle Tum! (book), 143
Timmers, Leo, 129
"Tiny Tim the Turtle" (song), 124
Titherington, Jean, 41
Tom and Pippo on the Beach (book), 59
Trains, Planes, and Automobiles (rhyme), 129
Truck Jam! (book), 129
tube monkey (craft), 60
Tugga Tugga Tugboat (book), 129
Turtle Day (book), 123
Turtle Splash! (book), 123
Twinkle, Twinkle, Little Star (book), 83
Two Little Black Birds (rhyme), 83
Two Little Redbirds (rhyme), 13

"Under the Sea" (song), 18

Valentine Hearts (rhyme), 36
Valentine in a Box (rhyme), 35

Van Laan, Nancy, 1, 14, 17, 143
Van Rynbach, Iris, 41
The Very Best Daddy of All (book), 65
The Very Hungry Caterpillar (book), 143
Vipont, Elfrida, 134

Waddell, Martin, 13, 123
Walsh, Ellen Stoll, 95
Walsh, Melanie, 27, 75
Watanabe, Shigeo, 56, 65, 143
Water, Water (book), 91
Watt, Fiona, 1, 101, 111, 117, 133
We Can Jump (rhyme), 56
Weatherford, Carole Boston, 75
Weeks, Sarah, 101
Wellington, Monica, 23
Wells, Rosemary, 1
We're Going on a Safari (book), 27
We've All Got Bellybuttons! (book), 55
What a Good Lunch! (book), 143
What Does Baby Say? (book), 133
What Shall We Do with the Boo-Hoo Baby? (book), 133
What the Sun Sees (book), 91
"What'll I Do with the Baby-O?" (song), 134
"Wheels on the Bus" (song), 76, 130
Where Is Baby's Belly Button? (book), 133
Where Is Baby's Mommy? (book), 71

Where Is Baby's Pumpkin? A Lift-the-Flap Book (book), 41
Where Is Baby's Valentine? (book), 35
Where Is the Green Sheep? (book), 95
"Where Oh Where Has My Little Dog Gone?" (song), 102
Where's My Daddy? (book), 65
Where's My Daddy? (flannel-board story), 66
Where's Spot? (book), 101
Who Is Driving? (book), 129
Who Says Woof? (book), 75
"Who Stole the Cookies?" (song), 144
Whose Baby Am I? (book), 133
Whose Chick Are You? (book), 13
Whybrow, Ian, 75
The Wide-Mouthed Frog: A Pop-Up Book (book), 123
Wiggle (book), 109
Willems, Mo, 1
Williams, Sue, 55
Wilson, Karma, 111, 117
Wojtowycz, David, 7, 75, 129
Wood, Audrey, 17, 55, 109
Wood, Don, 111
Wu, Norbert, 17

Yaccarino, Dan, 109
Yellow, Blue, and Bunny, Too! (book), 95
Yolen, Jane, 23, 111, 123

About the Author and Illustrator

Diane Briggs is a graduate of the School of Information Science at the State University of New York, Albany, and has worked in public and school libraries for eighteen years. She is the owner of Library Games, an online business located at www.librarygames.net, and has created two library game CD-ROMs: *I Love Books* and *Library Lollapalooza*. These are designed for librarians, parents, and educators to use with school-age children.

Briggs is the author of five other books: *Preschool Favorites: 35 Storytimes Kids Love*; *101 Fingerplays, Stories, and Songs to Use with Finger Puppets*; *52 Programs for Preschoolers*; *Toddler Storytime Programs*; and *Flannel Board Fun*.

Thomas Briggs is a student at Hudson Valley Community College in Troy, New York, where he is studying fine arts.

MAY 2009